MW00873430

Sweetness Begets Sweetness

© 2019

Karen DeBord Phillips

As Sweet as it gets!
Karen

ISBN: 9781798820001

Cover Photo by Karen DeBord Phillips

Sweetness Begets Sweetness

This book is dedicated to my sister Sherry and my brother Michael with special thanks to their spouses, John and Lisa.
And to Jack.

Special love and kudos to Marge, a true and loyal friend of the family.

Forward

It has been five years since Mom died. I had saved many of my notes and the emails that I exchanged with my siblings regarding mom's health. After her diagnosis with Alzheimer's disease, we scrambled to understand some of our family history and preserve it since it was fast slipping away as her brain became boggled.

It was only this year that I could re-read these notes and compile them into a book. This hopefully can serve as a family memory but also as a help to others we meet who are facing similar situations with a relative needing memory care.

Permission is granted to copy and use this to support and help others facing caregiving struggles with a loved one experiencing memory loss.

2019

Introduction

Mom taught me many valuable lessons, some of them having to do with daily tasks, some about relating to others, some about being self-determined and others just for fun. She was one of the most efficient and independent people I have ever known. She set the example for me about living and ultimately about dying.

As the middle child among three children in our family, she would use (what seemed at the time) tired axioms to press us into compliant behavior toward each other in the family. Since the family is the practice ground for later life, this was where we first learned about how to get along. One of these axioms was "sweetness begets sweetness." Similar to the Golden Rule, of course, it is true. She also taught us efficiency; for example to carry something up (or down) the stairs as you go; plan ahead, and don't procrastinate. We were taught to have a project ready for school days before it was due and not wait until the night before. We were taught to be clean and look neat in our appearance; be a good friend, and to be kind to each other (meaning my brother and sister).

But childhood wasn't all sweet and rule tendering. I also recall being spanked with a fly swatter, being told to wait until "your father gets home," being locked out of the house for hours to play in the yard and, (of all things) to drink out of the water hose instead of being allowed to go inside. Though these practices seemed appalling to me as a child, the end results have not been all that bad. She was a

dedicated mother. When I was sick, she sat by my
bed and read *Reader's Digest* jokes. When I got third
degree burns on vacation, she sat in the back seat
and fanned me all the way home.

Now that I am reaching by 65th birthday, I find myself
reflecting more on her life as I predict the ultimate
patterns of my life. She lived to be 84 years old. And,
although I thought our lives were different, as I age,
it seems they were more similar than I ever knew.
Maybe I am writing this memoir for fear I will lose
my memory and forget these life lessons.

In her final years, Mom presented a strong front as
that same woman who instructed us, disciplined us,
and cared for us when we were young, but began to
lose her memory. This proud and capable woman
was a victim of Alzheimer's. The tables turned and
this strong, independent woman was forced to
become dependent in her final years.

This is a story of my mom. It is written to honor the
woman she was and dedicated to my two siblings
whose support with decisions and final care were
essential. Being the middle child, I always felt left
out by my older sister and annoyed by my younger
brother. Now, I can't imagine having accomplished
this considerable caregiving task without them.

Chapter 1
Mom's Story as We Have Learned It

Margaret Ann Grindstaff was born in Kingsport, Tennessee on March 22, 1930. She was the only child of Laura Sue Clamon and Charles Coleman Grindstaff. Our family often refers to the "Clamon blood" as that which lends strength and a robust disposition to our family.

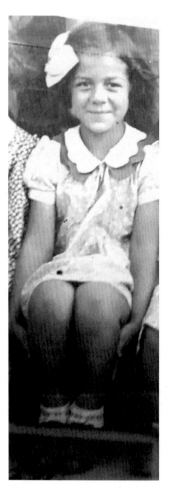

Although my grandfather was named Charles, my grandmother had a pet name for him that we all used: Bookey (pronounced Boo-key). Sue and Bookey were a totally enmeshed couple entwining themselves in one another's arms, reading the Bible together in bed, and spending the day working together in a hardware store that they owned. It seemed as if there was little room for their precious little girl, Margaret Ann.

Once, Mom told me a story about her childhood. Apparently, at about 5 years old, she was sitting on her daddy's lap in church. Her mother shamed her, telling her that she was too old to sit on his lap and that it must stop. That was but one example of how Mom tried to get close to her father but was not really allowed. Mom didn't feel like she was really part of them. Sue and Bookey were a single unit. Mom remained an only child left on the outside.

Since Mom was an only child, she was close with her Clamon (Grandmother's maiden name) cousins. She loved cousin Ray dearly as well as his sisters, Wilma, Jean, and JoAnn. There is an interesting story about Mom and Wilma riding in the back of Bookey's car when Mom was six years old. There was a "rumble seat" in their 1931 Studebaker. Rumble seats were placed in the trunk area of the car. Apparently as Bookey was driving on the Rotherwood Bridge in Kingsport, TN, the bridge collapsed. She and Wilma were in the rumble seat. The car was hanging off the edge of the bridge but Bookey was able to back up the car so they were able to exit the car safely. As mom tells it, a reporter came upon the scene after Bookey had so carefully backed the car off the bridge. The reporter was insisting on a photo with the car at the edge of the bridge. I don't think Bookey complied.

After Mom left for college, Sue and Bookey bought a talking parakeet named Dickey Boy. That bird got a great deal of their attention. I remember Dicky Boy calling me on my birthday when I was a child and singing *Happy Birthday*. I came to learn that they paid more attention to that little bird than they had to Mom.

Mom's feelings of being an outsider were evident as she went through a period feeling that she must have been adopted. Her mother, Laura Sue Clamon was insistent that she had given birth to Margaret Ann but she still felt insecure and apparently didn't

trust her mother. Locating the hospital records where she was born was her first thought. But it turned out the hospital and all of the records had burned in a fire. That didn't help her mother build a case that indeed she was born of Laura Sue and Bookey. Mom eventually did locate some photographs of Grandmother when she was pregnant and wrote to the write to the records department of the state of Tennessee for her birth certificate. Besides this evidence, Mom looked so much like Laura Sue!

In high school, Mom was a majorette and played clarinet in the band. Her best friend was Betty Jo Kress.

Her high school sweetheart was Bud Bullis.   She kept in touch with Betty Jo and Bud over the years and many of her Dobyns Bennett High School friends. I found her old high school yearbook from Kingsport, TN and even learned more; that she was in the senior play, a mixed chorus, on the yearbook staff, was a hospital aide, in the Spanish club, band and Home Economics Club.

Following high school, she attended East Tennessee State University for two years. I am not sure what she was taking in college but it could have been secretarial science. I know for a fact that she took great shorthand; a lost art today!

During her second year of college, her life changed. She met the man who eventually became my father. They were so in love. She dropped out of college and then Margaret Ann was married to Joseph Gordon Brown. She had learned to sew and made her own satin wedding dress. It was a work of art! To this day, I still have the beautiful wedding dress complete with over 50 satin covered buttons down the back and up each sleeve.

Establishing Her New Family
Dad went on to complete four years of college and plus his Master's Degree. He became an elementary school principal at Springbrook High School in Alcoa, Tennessee. Mom stayed home, kept house, and gave birth to two daughters who were three years apart; first born, Sheridan Lynn and second born, Karen Sue (that's me!).

In 1957, after serving as a principal for 7 years, Gordon was offered the position of Dean of Men at Emory and Henry College in Emory, Virginia. Emory's steady population of 354 is a rural community nestled in southwest Virginia. The Methodist College offered faculty housing. So the Brown family moved into a 4-bedroom house across the railroad tracks from the college.

In Emory, social life centered on friendships and Mom nurtured those through church, volunteer work through our schools, and bridge clubs. The pace of life was slower then and the telephone was a rather new invention. Telephone chatting became a past time for many housewives at that time who talked for hours on the phone—Mom included. This

was during the time when party lines were still in use so Mom and Lois Hill tied up the line even though they were just a stone's throw away as neighbors!

Michael Gordon was born to Margaret and Gordon while living in Emory in the closest hospital in Abingdon, VA. Mike's birth completed the family with each child spaced three years apart. Sherry and Karen attended Meadowview Elementary through fourth and seventh grade respectively. In 1964, Gordon was offered a promotion to become Dean of Men at a much larger university. The family moved to Blacksburg, VA where he also served in other administrative positions with Virginia Polytechnic Institute. He held such titles as Dean of Men, Dean of

Student Services, Director of Housing and Placement Coordinator. The university grew and its name grew as well, becoming Virginia Polytechnic Institute and State University, later abbreviated to Virginia Tech.

As the children grew, the girls became involved in band, athletics, drama, and made many close friends, while Mike took on a paper route, joined boy scouts and was all about football. Mom stayed home, cooked, cleaned and socially was referred to as Mrs. J. Gordon Brown. Not unlike other women supporting their husband's position, Mom seemed to lose her own identity as she fulfilled the wifely role. Mom was a good cook and an organized entertainer.

By the time Karen and Mike were both in high school, Mom got restless and needed to pursue something outside the home. She started first by brushing up on her shorthand and typing skills. Her first paid job was a part time job-sharing secretarial position at the Methodist church that we attended. This half-day job, shared with Doris Welch, allowed her to be home to meet Karen & Mike getting off the bus in the afternoons. Sherry often stayed late after school with band or drama club.

After gaining confidence in this position, she moved on to work at the Virginia Tech Bookstore in the office. It was during this time that it was evident that Mom and Dad were growing apart. It was the 1970's —an era of bra-burning and women's liberation, but Mom's eyes also were opened to the fact that she was smart and strong on her own and was tired of being Mrs. J. Gordon Brown. We later discovered that she felt she saw Dad as controlling and a tight-fisted bread earner. She was expected to not only stretch a monthly household allowance but to also serve as the wife of a man in a powerful position. Although a good man, Gordon had conveyed that he was the head of the family and felt power in his bread-earning role.

As a family with only one car, this left Mom at home without transportation. Dad's morning routine was to drop me and my sister off at the high school, drive to work, come home, watch the news or mow the lawn, read a bit (usually *Time* magazine), then go to bed. On Monday's he would go to a Rotary meeting and I can remember mom often making breakfast for dinner (omelets or pancakes).

What did Mom do all day? Well, our house was spotless and sometimes when we got home from school she had sewn us a new dress to wear to school. Of course the fabric had to come out of that monthly allowance Dad gave to her.

By the time Sherry was married, Karen off to college, and Mike had moved out on his own, then Mom moved into Mike's old bedroom. She explained that Dad snored and kicked her in his sleep. We believed that story for a while, but then noted that they didn't even communicate and didn't go places together very often. Dad kept busy with work. For at least 10 years, the two co-existed in the house for the good of "the children."

When I was in college, I recall going home on college breaks and having to visit Mom in her quarters and telling her about my life; then dad separately. They were like two ships in the night, not speaking. One Christmas we were all at home but had to have two shifts of gift giving as they would not share the same room. There was not arguing, just ignoring one another. This routine was becoming more and more stressful for us and most likely for them. Once we had each established some semblance of an adult life, Dad decided he should move out. Mom had noticed Dad packing a few things at a time but

he had not communicated with her about his plans. After Dad moved into his little one bedroom apartment we were all stressed. I remember Mom's bitterness and financial needs. She even asked me to take sides but I refused to do so knowing that would alienate everyone at some point. Since it was their private relationship, I had no idea who was right and who was wrong. Although Dad left her the house, no alimony was paid. Her income was very low as an office worker. Her parents were very supportive on the phone during this time and were worried about Mom.

Dad's supervisor at Virginia Tech was a good family friend with whom we had spent many holidays and picnics. Mom was a good friend with his wife. They played bridge, socialized, and exchanged Christmas gifts. However, he became counselor to Mom during this new phase, coaching her and helping boost and build her confidence. This of course, alienated Dad from him at work making his life difficult and pressing Dad into eventual early retirement.

It was during this time (the late 1970's) that Mom applied for and moved into the position of secretary for (then) football Coach, Bill Dooley. Her job was to type and maintain the play books, support the assistant coaches, book travel for recruiting trips, communicate with player's parents, and generally to be available throughout the week, on game days, and go so far as to host gatherings for the parents of players.

Mom stayed active in her attendance at the Methodist Church, played bridge, met friends (Flo, Marge, Carla, Doris, and others) for dinner, started walking several miles a day, dieted, went to movies, swam at the public pool, attended sporting events, and shopped. Indeed she was becoming her own woman. She was attractive and dressed well as she was the front door and first impression for Virginia Tech football office. Of course she had to look good as the coach's front line assistant, and accordingly, her shoe and clothing collection grew. She was a bargain hunter, even shopping consignment stores and yard sales!

As an emerging professional, whenever I needed upscale clothing, I would go through her wardrobe to find a new outfit and she was graciously willing to share. When the Home Shopping Network came out on television, she started ordering things from them...big things like a new vacuum cleaner. It was the first time she had money and was in control of it herself.

In the 1980's, Mike and I were both married and starting families. Sherry had married in the early 70's and had a son named Tony. Mom traveled to each of our homes and was a part of our lives. Dad became a single man and eventually remarried Patsy in the late 80's. We were able to get to know him a little better. His supervisor, who was still one of Mom's primary confidants, was making Dad's work at Virginia Tech difficult and he eventually took early retirement and he and my stepmother moved to Florida. About 1993, he discovered and was treated for prostate cancer. Short of their 10th wedding anniversary and his 65th birthday, he died as the cancer had spread to his bones and lungs.

Mom kept building on the positive aspects of being independent. She traveled with friends, even taking a cruise or two. We invited her to travel with our families as we visited each other to places like

Boston where Sherry lived, Virginia Beach where Mike lived, and Missouri where I moved for a while. We had a fun vacation once when we took her to Branson, Missouri and saw Mel Tillis in concert. She was truly independent and loving it and we enjoyed her company!

Chapter 2
Her Newfound Independence

After my daughter, Whitney was born, I lived in Blacksburg not far from Mom while I was working on my Ph.D. at Virginia Tech. During that time Mom's parents' were still living in Florida. Their health had started to decline. Since Mom was an only child, I became her support system helping her make some tough decisions about their care. Grandmother and Bookey were burdening their neighbors with calls for help and tasking the ambulance service with calls to be taken to the emergency room. They were not eating well, losing weight, and declining. Mom had to step into action. Mom was organized and could get a lot accomplished! Within a matter of two weeks, she traveled to Florida, cleaned out and sold their house, and flen them back to Virginia to live in the Showalter Center of Warm Hearth Village in Blacksburg.

She was working fulltime in the football office, but she often was called away to take Grandmother or Bookey to the doctor's office. Because I was in graduate school and had two young children, she and I found that we were sandwiched between her parents and my young children.

By that time, there were five grand children: Sherry's son, Tony Hume; Mike's two children Katie & Garrett Brown and my children Whitney & Shawn DeBord. She gave them gifts, celebrated their birthdays, and traveled with us as we moved from Blacksburg to Harrisonburg, VA, Orlando, FL, Boston, MA, Virginia Beach, Floyd, VA, Columbia, MO and Raleigh, NC.

Between Sherry, Mike and I, there were also stepchildren and we negotiated eight marriages. With this expanding family, divorce, marriage, remarriage, confirmations, christenings, weddings, and family gatherings were rather frequent. But it was always family times when we all enjoyed each other the most.

Mom continued to work and was the Administrative Assistant to Coach Frank Beamer, a long time winning football coach at Virginia Tech. She became friends with many of the families of the players and was responsible for booking Frank's recruiting trips as well as attending to details when a bowl game was involved. She had items from many of these

bowls such as a Sugar Bowl watch, an Orange bowl sweat suit and more. She was a true Hokie! But in her free time, she continued to play bridge, meet up with friends, and be involved with our families as much as was possible.

In addition to being a working woman, Mom was supportive of me. By now I was completing my doctoral dissertation and working part time. Whitney was five years old and a year before my graduation, my son Shawn was born. Mom helped throw a post-birth baby shower and she hosted a graduation party for me. At the same time, she was enduring the stress as her parent's caregiver. Only about a year after we moved Grandmother and Bookey from Florida, he suffered a few strokes. But one day, he just died. No long illness or sudden attack, he just died. Grandmother was heart broken. She even had a short stint in the hospital with unexplainable delusions and confusion.

After Bookey's death, I noticed that she and mom easily angered each other. She called Mom a nickname, *Marthy*, which mom didn't seem to mind, but behind her back she sometimes told me that Mom was a "bitch!" That didn't sit well with me, as I knew the load that Mom was carrying with work and her caregiving as an only child.

Living in the Showalter Center, Grandmother had her meals in the cafeteria and often there were activities she enjoyed. She enrolled in a writing class for elders conducted by the famous writer and faculty member at Virginia Tech, Nikki Giovanni. She wrote several stories from her past including the one about the rumble seat and several stories about Dickey Boy, their bird. One particularly funny story was about how she and Bookey had carefully applied new wallpaper in their house. Upon awakening the next morning, they found it had all fallen off the walls. This and other writings led us to believe that Grandmother was managing Bookey's death well through this therapeutic writing.

Later that year, Mom and Grandmother took Mom's car and followed Ted and me with Whitney and

Shawn, to Virginia Beach for Christmas (1991).
Complete with baby seat and supplies, we could not
all ride together and had to take two cars. It was a 6-
hour ride to Mike's house. As with many families
during the holidays, there was a bit of family drama.
I don't recall what it was about, but the day after
Christmas, Grandmother somehow angered Mom
and they ended up leaving a day early. When they
got home, Mom delivered Grandmother back to the
Showalter Assisted Living Center. Apparently after
that, Grandmother sat down and wrote her thank-
you notes to each of us for the gifts and time
together. Our kid-caravan arrived home the
following day.

The next day, Mom's good friend Marge called to tell
me that Mom had taken grandmother to the hospital
for an unknown reason. I drove down to
Montgomery Regional hospital to see what was
going on (it was before cell phones).

When I arrived at the hospital, there sat Mom in a
chair with a blank look on her face. And there lay
Grandmother, still warm, in the hospital bed. She
had died as they sat waiting for the doctor. We
always figured it was from a broken heart, living life
without Bookey. Her thank-you note arrived the
next day. Bookey had died on June 28, 1990 and
Grandmother on Dec. 31, 1991.

Chapter 3
A New Phase- Dating Again!

Without the caregiving responsibility, Mom could now have a bit of freedom to travel and not feel as if she had to be close by to care for Grandmother. She attended a high school class reunion in Tennessee. After living over 20 years as a divorcee, Mom reunited with her high school sweetheart, Bud Bullis. They still were very attracted to each other. Later that fall, Bud and his faithful dog traveled all the way from South Dakota in his camper to visit Mom in Blacksburg. Wherever Bud went, so did his loyal

 dog. Mom, Bud, and the dog traveled together that summer to another high school reunion and later that season took a cross-country trip in the camper.

Even though she adored Bud, after a three-week trip in an RV camper with the dog, she decided that this was not the life she wanted. She got on a plane and came home early. I picked her up at the Raleigh airport. She stayed in touch with Bud and some of his close friends in South Dakota. It was those close friends who brought her the news of Bud's death. He had been found dead in a one-car accident on a long stretch of road near his home in South Dakota.

Nobody knew how long he had been there but his
loyal dog was lying right beside him.
That was sort of a turning point it seemed to a new
phase of Mom's life. No more looking into the past.

In about 2003, out of the blue, she had a phone call
asking her for a date! It was Dr. Gregory, our family
dentist. Having suffered through the caregiving of
his wife, who eventually died of cancer, he was ready
for female companionship. He needed a date for a
holiday function and his receptionist suggested
Margaret Brown saying, "She's a nice looking woman
and has a good personality. Ask her out!" So Greg
invited her to a Christmas party and she accepted.
Their first date, his front car door was jammed and
she had to ride in the back seat while he
chauffeured. Mom good-naturedly climbed into the
back seat!

Greg loved to travel and enjoyed Mom's company.
Together they enjoyed traveling to Turkey, Russia,
Nova Scotia, Europe, Hawaii, domestic bus trips to
places like Monticello and Gatlinburg, TN and river
cruises on the Danube and Mississippi Queen. The
accompanied each other to grand children's
graduations, weddings, and christenings.

Mom was having fun dating Greg. They often
entertained in our old home place on Locust Avenue
or at his house across town. By that time, my first
husband, Ted and I had grown apart and had gotten
divorced. Having been in my shoes, Mom was very
supportive of me during the separation and our
ultimate divorce. This life event seemed similar to
Mom's, but the difference was that I never grew

bitter toward Ted and we had a rather friendly divorce. It still felt a little like history repeating itself. Mike and Sherry may have felt the same way as they too, experienced divorces!

After a few years (much like Mom), I started dating. I wanted Mom to meet my new love interest, Jack. We went too Blacksburg to my childhood home on Locust Avenue. The first night Jack met Mom; we were in the living room having a glass of wine. Mom's good friend, Marge had just become engaged to Travis and all was festive. During conversation, laughter and fun, Mom realized that Greg could not remember her birthdate. Jokingly, she said if he didn't remember it that she would just have to "pour wine on his head." In a fun, but sort of weird moment, she indeed drizzled a few drops of wine over his head while Jack and I along with Marge and Travis looked on. Mom always needed to be in

charge and be "right!" Anything that was not going "her way" led to confrontations. We laughed it off but reflect on that moment now and wonder.

We always called my stepfather Dr. Gregory since he had been our dentist. Sometimes we referred to him our step dentist and sometimes we would call him

"Greg," as Mom did. He was accepted as part of our family and the grand children grew up knowing "Greg." He was there for Christmas and Thanksgiving alternating with his family.

After a few years of dating Greg, Mom went to Virginia Beach to help care for Mike after a knee surgery. Greg missed her terribly and upon her return insisted they get married. Reverend Reggie Tuck married them after a Sunday service at the Methodist Church in Blacksburg. Her boss, the VA Tech Assistant Athletic Director, Tom Gabbard, and his wife served as witnesses. I sent her a party-favor that was a wedding veil I purchased at a party show. It was intended as a joke. I didn't think she would wear it! But later I saw some pictures of her wearing it. It seemed out of place. Even though we didn't comment on it then, now we reflect and wonder.

Mom's retirement years
By this time Mom had decided to retire from the Virginia Tech Athletic Department to spend more time with Greg. She continued to swim at the community center, play bridge, and they traveled together. She kept us up to date with their lives by writing emails to us. The adjustment of these two in-love retirees combining households and lives was a bit rocky as they learned each other's nuances.

Mom sold our childhood home and downsized. Greg gave his home to his son and together Mom and Greg bought a condo in the Vistas. Greg was still seeing dental patients 2-3 days a week but had sold his dental practice. He spent a great deal of time in front of the computer doing financial investments and continued to manage some rental properties. He loved gardening and had lovely grounds at his old house and also around the condo. He served on community boards and their lives were active.

Before great grandchild Destiny was born to my daughter Whitney, Mom had a bit of a tough time. She adored Whitney and was trying to reconcile her love for Whitney with who she feared was a poor selection of mate for her. With the counsel of Reggie Tuck the preacher, she was able to come to realize that baby Destiny was another gift from God and finally she accepted her whole-heartedly. Her shopping gene kicked in again and she bought about 20 little outfits for Destiny including a Virginia Tech cheerleading outfit. The next great grandchild was Mike's granddaughter Jaylyn followed by little sister Kendall. Then Shawn brought baby Jamison into the world, but she never had the chance to meet him.

Whitney's wedding occurred May 13, 2005, just 5 days before Destiny's birth. It was held in our lovely backyard in Raleigh. Mom and Greg attended and Mom was overindulging on wine. We sat on the deck on that May Day and watched as she leaned further into Greg. We realized she had consumed too much wine. My sister-in-law and I walked her up stairs to bed. As we undressed Mom to put her to bed, we noted her matching pink bra and panties and that even in her 70's that she looked quite stunning! But the overindulgence and how fast the wine affected her concerned us a bit.

When Greg turned 80, Mom hosted a very nice party on a Sunday afternoon in the press box of Lane

Stadium at VA Tech. Both sides of the family were there in addition to many friends from around Blacksburg. It was then that I felt as if the Gregory family had not really accepted her. It also was one of

the last times I recall her planning and event and entertaining.

In 2006, Mom turned 76. Sherry, Mike, and I decided to plan a surprise birthday party. We had some how missed the milestone year of 75, so we plotted to come up with a something unique and memorable. Mom had become part of the Red Hat society and she had a closet full of red hats. We planned a little Red Hat scavenger hunt surprise. We went through her Red Hats in her closet and decided that wearing red hats would be fun for us! We each arrived with our spouses from VA Beach, Raleigh, NC, and Jacksonville, FL.

The six of us assembled at mom's (ever faithful) friend Marge's house to go over the plan. We had fun trying on, then wearing her red hats to the party. Greg was in on the birthday secret and told Mom that they were going out for dinner. He played along by giving her the first clue to the scavenger hunt as a gift. After each clue, she would discover one of us as a prize. The clues took her all around the Virginia Tech campus. Mike and wife Lisa were waiting for her to find them at the War Memorial Chapel with a bottle of champagne in hand. Karen and husband

Jack were stationed at the Duck Pond. After these two discoveries, the caravan drove to the Farm House Restaurant to meet Travis and Marge for dinner. What they didn't know is that Sherry and husband John had also traveled in for the party from Florida. Mom cried we think in happiness but it also seemed as if she was a little baffled.

In a life where she had constructed a well-organized existence, where she was in charge, this seemed out of her control and she didn't seem comfortable. We sang to her, gave her gifts, and had fun. But all along, something seemed amiss. We reflect on that now and wonder.

Chapter 4
A Time of Questioning

We (three kids) noticed and discussed the fact that Mom had turned over so many of her newly discovered independent functions to Greg. She stopped cooking. They ate out more than cooked in. When they did eat in, Greg was often in charge of cooking. They had a housekeeper, so changing sheets and washing clothes was no longer her task to do. She continued to be able to manage routine chores like dish washing and folding the laundry. Greg had taken over bill paying and sat with Mom while she made out checks for her credit card purchases.

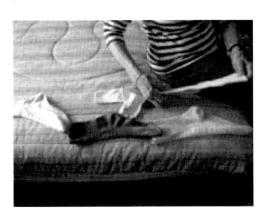

We began to question a few things. I saved a few of her emails that appeared truncated and often didn't make sense.

~~~~~

2007 from Mom to Karen
Bought the stuff for the eagle brand pie tomorrow. We will have company Saturday next June 9th. We went to three banks to get ready for money etc. for Russia. We had a great dinner last Thursday at Marshall Hunt's lovely home --- Pastor Reggie wants ---- MONEY, MONEY for the new St. Mary Church, Harding Avenue, our Church has purchased. Ugh --- I

do plan to give them some money but not tons -- both Greg and I will. Greg is giving up the Presbyterian Church and will join BUM Church! Yea --- it has taken 3 years to get him to want to do it.   Almost time for bed. Well will tell you about the pie. Love ya Hope Jack is OK. How was Shawn and Whitney?

~~~~~~~~~~~~
An email **From Karen to Mom**

> Mom-
> I made the eagle brand pie like your recipe below because that is what you had given to me. Eagle brand milk alone doesn't get firm. I tried to bake the cherry pie the other night for dinner and it was served in a bowl. Here is the recipe you sent to me.
> Margaret Gregory wrote:
>> Eagle Brand Cherry Pie
>> Buy Pie at store
>> 1 can eagle bran milk
>> 1 can tart cherries (drained)
>> 1/4 lemon juice
>> 1 t. almond extract
>> mix add to cooled shell - refrig. overnight

From Karen to Mike & Sherry
Mike & Sherry-
I am concerned about Mom and wanted to consider us talking about a strategy to discuss these concerns with them when Mom and Greg get back from Russia.

I mentioned Mom's memory loss to Greg and I don't really want to bring it up with Marge. I think it may be too personal at this point.

Jack and I plan to go to B'burg on the evening of July 9th to ride over with them on the 10th to Floyd, Virginia to see the work on Mike's new house. I could make an appointment with someone (a neurologist) for sometime while I am there and invite her to go with me for testing. She is telling us that all of her friends also forget stuff, but it seems to me that she seems to forget more. Jack's mom is 82 and doesn't do this. Think about others you know. Karen

To Karen from Sherry 6-07:
You know what? I have similar symptoms, don't you all? I don't seem to be as in tune to it as being a problem with mom as you are.

In my last conversation with Mom she said she was working on this herself. It is a sensitive issue and one best discussed with her in person one on one, but not to make her feel sick or dumb. Scheduling a doctor's appt. is a good idea if she agrees in advance, but do you want to ruin her vacation with your concerns now? Are you scaring Mom and Greg without actual medical support? Will you ruin a special time for Mike and Lisa by this being the center of discussion?

My vote is you not rush into this without more careful consideration and medical discussion, please. Sherry

From Karen to Mike & Sherry 9-07
When I talked with Mom today, she was unable to convey what Greg's biopsy results showed so

she put him on the phone. She said that her job is to keep him positive, which it is, but he is somewhat discouraged. What he has is called: Myelodysplastic Syndrome. I looked it up online and found a few links that I will send to you. It means that he has a low red blood count. In younger patients, they do bone marrow transplants. Greg said they recommended blood transfusions and iron supplements. But then they also said to do nothing for 6 weeks. I am not sure what to make of it but thought I would let you know what I found out. Karen

~~~~~~

In the fall of 2007, Mike, Lisa, Jack and I had tickets to a Saturday afternoon Virginia Tech football game. We stayed in the condo with Mom and Greg. I had talked with Greg over the phone and he was in agreement that Mom had some difficulties remembering things. My plan was to wait until Sunday breakfast to bring up the evidence of memory loss and the fact that she needed to see a doctor to provide any preventative care if she were diagnosed with a form of Alzheimer's. Mike, Lisa, and Greg agreed that we should bring it up and discuss it with Mom.

After the football game, somehow the topic came up anyway and Mom wanted to discuss it then. She brought out the tired story that all of her friends forget things too. I told her we could talk about it tomorrow but she insisted (as only Mom could) in discussing it _now_. At that point, I could not help it and I started to cry. I told her that I loved her and just wanted to look out for her best interest, which is why I felt we should see a doctor about it. She got out the phone book and asked me who she should see. Greg suggested a nice Physician's Assistant he had met named Carol Ballard. I asked Greg to help set up an appointment. I started by faxing a letter Ms. Ballard informing her that we had concerns about Mom's memory and wanted to have her advise us.

~~~~~~~~~

Excerpts from letter from Karen to Carol Ballard 11-07

…Her sentence structure in her emails is truncated and choppy. When she explains things in conversation she leaves out words leading to a guessing game and some frustration on her part trying to name common items. She often calls things by the wrong name (shoes for pants for example) and can't think of the name for common things (bus, football stadium) and has to describe it to us. Last week she was concerned about her cousin who has lung cancer and she called it "cancer lungs." She is aware of her memory issue and has agreed to discuss it with a doctor. I believe she has made this appointment with you to begin this discussion.

~~~~~~~~~

Email from Mom
12-07
Merry Christmas. Mine is all done!!! It is beautiful (if I say so). It was fun and I did not drag things from the 3 years we used before. It was to much work. I got things I wanted to do and I just love it. Lights are already showing from the outside on the BENCH. --- I used read gales to put around

the pillars for the porch. Just beautiful and I am really happy. The back out deck looks good also --- red etc. etc.. It is fun but I am done now. Monday, I will go to Mammogram (do it each year). Tuesday, Greg and the guys will play bridge that night. Wednesday, I will see Carol Ballard, Physical. Thursday, Greg and I go to SOB for dinner with friends -- Marge and Travis in Blacksburg. Friday I can go get my poor sick car. Only $100.00 --- it could have been $1,000.00 -- Yea. Saturday, Greg and I will go to Rotary in Blacksburg for dinner for a composer or a person who songs or plays professionally. Greg and I are going to Roanoke next Sunday after church and take Doris Welch for dinner. Ho Hum --- that is all the info I know now. The air is quite cole is bad and maybe snow tomorrow!!!!!!!!!! We love you guys. MERRY, MERRY ,MERRY!!!

~~~~~~~~~~
From Mom to Sherry, Karen & Mike
1-08
Guess your mother does not forget anything for her son and daughters --- how wonderful my lives have been with my three lovers. Take care. Greg and I went to see one of the doctors and she are so cute (she has 3 sons) and she will take us talking up tomorrow and will help me with names and numbers etc. Ho Ho. Life is something different. Snow is still every good here and it is very cold but the snow is beautiful. Love ya and all is good!!! Mom

~~~~~~~~~~~~~

The Physician's Assistant referred Mom to a neurologist, in Salem, Virginia. The conducted a PET scan. Mom was diagnosed with Alzheimer's. For the next appointment, I went along with she and Greg. I wanted to witness the examination myself. Dr. H was very patient with her. Mom fawned over him saying he was "good looking." During the exam, he asked her to spell several words backwards including ORANGE. That made even me a bit anxious, and I have practiced that little exercise over and over since! He asked her what day it was and who the

president was. At that time, Mom called President Obama "Oobie Doobie."

Each time Greg took Mom to the neurologist, they adjusted her medication first starting out with Aricept (which is common for new diagnoses). Next came Namenda, then the Exelon patch. Seroquil was added for moodiness along the way.

She had gone through a phase of being really moody. My brother began to call Greg "a saint" for putting up with her moods. She still kept herself clean and neat but her color choices and combinations in clothing had gotten a little strange.

Mom and Greg continued to go about their lives going out to eat, taking short trips on tour buses, and meeting friends. Occasionally she got "cross" with Greg and reflecting on it now, I think it was her frustration over not being able to express herself as eloquently as she once had.

Chapter 4
Stress Hastens the Disease Progression

For those who have lived in Blacksburg and anyone ever affiliated with Virginia Tech, the student shootings that occurred April 16, 2008 were a horrible tragedy. For those living in town, it was a stressful time with daily reminders in the newspapers, flags hung about town, memorials, flowers, and ceremonies. Mom saved every newspaper clipping. When I got to town a few days after the shootings, I saw that she had displayed these papers on the dining room table. She was rightfully stressed, but also she was obsessed. The culmination of the events of the past few years (her marriage, selling her house and moving, adjusting to living in a new home, retirement, and now the shootings) made it appear to me as if her memory issues had become more prevalent. She conveyed, "We had to go over to the place for a service." I asked what place that was. After floundering for the word, she finally came up with that place where they play basketball. "Ah, the coliseum!"

As things calmed in Blacksburg, we visited more and I observed Mom, always reporting back to Mike and Sherry. Mom so enjoyed sitting on the deck. One spring day when I was visiting, as we sat on the deck amongst the spring flowers, a butterfly darted about and she said, "Look at that pretty little thing." I said, "Mom what is that?" She said, "Wait – don't tell me. It's not a watermelon is it?" That made me laugh. And so we entered the funny stage of this disease. Over time as we saw her declining. Her emails were confusing. I was glad she was still using the computer! I am not sure why I saved these, but I thought that someday, I might need to explain the trajectory. They follow.

~~~~~~~~~~~~
6-08
Hey --- I has three ladies over to my home today from 1:00 until 5:00 and we had fun played bridge down strays.   I did not win. Ho Ho.   Each Monday, Wednesday, Friday I go to the Swimming Pool Contractors in Blacksburg --- close to our home -- 9.00 - 10.00.   "Jean" taught us how to take care of us --- it if fun in and the water and is not too cool.   I bought three suites and they are cute.   Greg went to his doctor today who shot his arm for more read blood. He will go over next Wednesday. He is a very good boy. Ray and Jewel called us a minutes ago to see how Greg is doing. He has been such a good boy today.   I told him I will take him out for dinner tonight!!!   We are having fun and looking for our trip Nova-Scotia –

7-09
I am a wonderful Mother since I have three children. What a great day having You and Jack at our Home. Hope we can be with you guys whenever you want in Blacksburg. I had lots of fun with both of you --- and Greg. All three of you can TALK. The rain is already wet --- we walked around this afternoon but the rain got us. Thank you for your note, Karen. I have always loved two

*girls and one boy --- all three THE BEST
CHILDREN in this world. You remembers all
my friends. I think about Emory lots of time.
I love your children and they love me. I can
see every day. I really do love Jack --- Greg
and I will keep him --- you also. Between
God and you and I --- know that the hove we
have because this is the way to live --- you
and I keep the children and our friends
because God told us how to live his
way. This is just what you and I live and
ready for God when he is ready for
us. Karen, I love you now and will
love you FOR EVER. Come home when
you can. You are a wonderful LADY.*
~~~~~~

Another email that was sent to Mike, Sherry, and me
was another example of the "humorous" stage of the
disease.
~~~~~~~

*Today is Monday, August 24, 2009. Shirley is
not working today. I have worked a lot
today. Pore Mom. Greg has gone to see Sports
Club to this evening. The guys love to talk two
hours together. It is very hot this afternoon. I
am sitting on the dick and it is very pretty. Hope
all of you are OK. Your Mother loves all of you.*
~~~~~~~~~~

Jack and Mike had to phone each other for a laugh
over that one! Of course she meant she was sitting
out on the deck.

When I told her I was going to retire and try to move
closer to her, this is the email she sent:
~~~~~~~~

10-09

I am so happy for you to stop working. You have been a good mother for your sweet two children. Also for Jack who is a lover for me and you. Ted is a very good man as far as I think.

I have some sweet children and mothers and daddies. Greg says congratulation for you. Now you can come to our house when you want to. I LOVE YOU SO MUCH.
~~~~~~~~~

After I retired from North Carolina State University in December 2009, I taught adjunct at Virginia Tech for the Spring 2010 semester. I stayed with Mom and Greg for a couple of weeks. I was teaching an online class, but I had planned to be in class the first two weeks to get to know the students. I discovered that the students preferred to actually learn at a distance instead of meeting me in the classroom so I conducted the rest of the class from our home near Raleigh, NC.

While I was staying in Blacksburg for the first two weeks of the semester, I set up my office on a card table in the guest room of Mom and Greg's condo. One day, I decided to cook for them. I prepared several dishes to put into two-person serving containers and freeze, carefully labeling them for Greg to warm in the oven. I asked her to help me thinking this would be an activity that she would enjoy. When I asked her to find me a can opener, she opened all of the kitchen drawers and asked, "Is it one of these? I don't know what it looks like." She then pointed to the microwave and stove and said, "I don't know what these things do any more." That was more descriptive than I had ever read or heard to have an understanding how her brain was failing her.

During those weeks, I even thought I might start to sing with the church choir as I had when I lived in Blacksburg before. I took Mom to rehearsal with me one night and she sure enjoyed listening and humming along. She had always loved music! During that time, I observed Mom and Greg on behalf on Sherry and Mike. I kept a little journal of my observations. I guess the journal was somewhat therapeutic for me to keep and also to inform my family what I was seeing.
~~~~~~~~~

1-30-2010
I am teaching a class via distance education at Virginia Tech this semester. I decided I would come to Blacksburg and teach in person for 2 weeks. I am staying with Mom and Greg. It has been an interesting experience as they are both aging almost right before my eyes. He had a fall last week requiring 8 stitches in his head. This shook him up and upset mom a great deal. This weekend it snowed, and she was fearful he would go outside and by chance fall again but we all stayed inside. I have made several observations about them individually and together.

Greg is very routine-oriented. He gets up, makes coffee and reads the paper for nearly 3 hours before retreating to the basement. Mom says he is "watching the paper." Going to the basement is like going to work. He spends hours in his basement office filing papers, monitoring his stocks, calling brokers, and making land deals. Sometimes he naps and sometimes he reads more of the paper. He keeps busy in his own little world and she misses him when he is down there. Much of the time he spends in the basement is an escape from house tiding, questioning, and telling him how to act. He doesn't hear well, so when she asks him a question and he doesn't quite have the correct words, he wants her to repeat it. He looks at her and scowls in an effort to understand. Then she feels hurt thinking he doesn't care. He thinks she is irritable and they both seem to irritate each other over small things (such as the volume on the television remote).

While Greg is in the basement, Mom stays upstairs and watches movies on TV. With her waning memory, it is difficult for her to do much productive work. She is very good at cleaning and washing dishes. She can't identify simple appliances by name in the kitchen but knows not the function of most of them. She can't follow a recipe and simply says, "I just don't do that anymore." She can't identify a nickel from a penny but knows they are both money. She has a hard time retaining the spelling of words in her head so we have to spell things very slowly for her. Her handwriting is still much better than most. Yesterday I was hoping we could have a good time cooking together in the kitchen. Most of the time, she kept asking me why I was doing "all this?" I told her I enjoyed it and if she didn't want to be a part of it to go in the other room. But she DID want to be a part of it and washed up every pot and pan I dirtied. She was very helpful in this way and commented several times, I used to do all this" and indeed she did. Greg sat at the table reading the paper, snickering every once in awhile as I bantered back and forth with her. I was able to put together several dishes to freeze for them to each in the future (navy beans and cornbread, chili, beef stroganoff, chicken pot pie, and hamburger pie).

Often Mom will pull out old photographs and letters. She looks at the faces to identify them as if she is struggling to recall. Most of the time she has written their names by their picture and that helps. Yesterday we spent about 2 hours doing this. Today we did a similar activity for about an hour. Sometimes she doesn't know the people in the photos and asks who they are. She pulled out her wedding pictures with Dad. Greg said she had asked him who these people were and of course he was not there and doesn't know. Mom and Dad were divorced over 20 years ago. He died in 1993. But before and during their divorce, she grew to hate him. Now she looks at the photos of him and says how she "loved him" and that he "was a good guy". She has list after list, phone number after phone number written in multiple locations. She looks at these lists, again in an effort to not let these people slip through her memory.

With Alzheimer's disease, sections of the brain seem to be atrophying. For her, it is not short term versus long term so much as the prefrontal lobe can no longer process information. Descriptive words are missing, as is the ability to organize thoughts in her head to take action (recipes, computer functions, etc.). She can put away a whole dishwasher full of dishes in the correct locations but she cannot remember who the person on the phone is when they call and cross reference that with the context in which she may have known them.

I have had discussions with Mom and Greg separately and then together to ask them what we should do for alternative living arrangements should one or both of them need more healthcare attention in the near (or far) future. Tomorrow we are going to visit a retirement center. If Mom and Greg have to downsize from 3000 square feet to 1000 square feet it will be so difficult. I feel that the activity outlets for Mom in such a place would be good. She is an extrovert and she needs human interaction. Greg, being more of an introvert, needs quite time. Perhaps a new arrangement can prolong their time with us even longer.
~~~~~
1-31-10
Mom's house is a booby trap with little trinkets placed about. She knows where each item is. There are little Mardi Gras necklaces on the door for decoration but they jangle when one gets up in the night. These trinkets are in a very specific order. Keeping order must be a way to maintain control and lessen confusion. I have learned to never turn the computer monitor to allow others to see the screen. The cord is too short and the monitor goes off. Then she thinks we have messed things up. I was using plastic storage containers for the food I had been preparing. As I was putting them back into the

garage on the shelf where they belonged, I dropped them. No big deal, but they made a sound. She came running and fussing.

There is a metal cooking sheet in the microwave oven. Do you think I would ever move that out? Each time the computer monitor went off or the dishes dropped, the exclamation of "Don't do that. Leave it alone! Ask me if and I will do it. You don't know how to do it!" I told her just to "stop it now." It is no big deal but to her, it must sound like a cymbal crashing and rock her world! I think we are not in the "humorous" stage of this disease any longer!

Yesterday, we went to the mall and she seemed to enjoy that. She stopped and looked at each rack. She even purchased a jacket that was on sale. It was good to get her out. Even with snow on the road, the main roads were all cleared. I had cleared my windshield from the 11 inches of snow that had accumulated on my car. The hood of the car however had a mound of snow still on it. Once we went down the first hill, all of that snow slid down and blocked my vision. I had to pull over to get it off. But then the wipers were jammed. Mom tried to tell me what to do about it. She told me to go to "this place" and have the "man look at it." I think she meant Jiffy Lube, but it was closed. After all, it was Sunday. Thankfully they started working in the next block.

~~~~~~

2-1-10

Today the three of us visited Warm Hearth Village including touring the Showalter Health Care Center which is part of Warm Hearth. At

Showalter, there are social activities, hairdressers, a dentist, cafeteria-served meals, and transportation assistance. Those who live in this center are given priority to be able to transition into the Krontjee memory care center for a continuum of care. The entire property is lovely and is "secure." But, I got a glimpse of the drama that will occur if they move.

There is the option to split Mom and Greg up their care needs would be different. But this is where the conversation turned sour. Mom liked the property until the consultant started saying, "Now, if she goes over to Memory Care, then you can visit." Or, "you can stay here or go too—couples do it both ways." Mom looked sternly at Greg and said, "I will not do this alone, Mister!" We smoothed it over, but I definitely heard her and felt for her! We went ahead and put them on the waiting list anyway and took the packet of materials with pricing and unit floor plans. The consultant advised us to go ahead with a move if possible and not wait until a crisis. I agree. This is not easy! But I agree that pre-planning is critical!

End of Journaling.

Chapter 5
Losing Independence

Mom was still driving her car and I must say some rides were a little scary. One day, she had driven down the street to the pool to swim class. The pool was just a straight shot down the road from her condo, so it was an easy half-mile there and back. A friend asked for a ride home and Mom complied. However, once in the woman's neighborhood, she could not figure out how to get back home. I can only imagine the sense of panic. She finally got out of the neighborhood and found a fast food restaurant. The manager called Greg and he had to come to get her. After that little event, Mike and Lisa gave Mom a little keychain that looked like a fire hydrant. It was a canister in which Mike had typed up her name, address, and in case of emergency phone numbers to present if she ever needed it. Even though her car continued to be parked in their garage that was the last time she drove. Later she admitted that she didn't know what each part (like the wipers) did in the car.

That spring, Jack and I flew to Blacksburg in our small plane to see Mom and Greg. Jack has a small homebuilt plane (RV-4) and it was far quicker to make the 50-minute trip from Raleigh in the plane than drive 4 hours to see them. That day, the weather reports were clear but by the time we got over Blacksburg, a huge bank of clouds enveloped us. It was a whiteout, so Jack immediately started climbing to a higher altitude where it was clear and there was visibility. I started praying. We stayed above the clouds until we could see the ground below through an opening in the clouds. Jack was able to spiral down to the airport below and land safely. Once on the ground, Mom hugged me and felt me shaking from fear I felt during the flight. I told her in brief that it was cloudy up there and that I got a little scared. She soothed me and my Mom's loving arms were around me and I needed her in that moment!

Greg's health continued to decline and he even said that the doctors indicated that he was the longest living patient with his condition. I felt as if they were keeping each other going. Their weeks were made up of doctor's appointments and Mom became ever so dependent upon Greg. On separate occasions Greg and then Pastor Reggie called me trying to tell me that Greg was getting sicker and asking what I was "going to do about Mom." Are you kidding me? I replied, "What ever happened to the vow of for better or worse, and in sickness and in health? " I was livid that this was my responsibility to take her and possibly take her away from Greg. Can you imagine tangling with a wild cat mama were I to take her away from Greg?

Greg determined that he needed help at home and he enlisted the help of the caregiver. He contacted Jeannie who had looked after his dying wife years before. Jeannie was a godsend and her staff of 2-3 other caregivers came up with a schedule starting with 2 days a week and working up to 7 days a week over time. It seemed that their main responsibility was to be a companion for Mom and keep her out of Greg's way. He had business downstairs on the computer with his investments (plus it was his escape) and the caregiver did light housework and sat and watched TV with Mom upstairs.

When I visited, I would do my class planning while watching movies with Mom. I took her shopping, or we would just walk around the mall and look at things. She loved getting out since her outings otherwise were to Greg's doctors where she loyally sat while he received transfusions. She loved him and cared for him as he lost bowel and bladder control as a side effect from the chemo he was receiving. The caregivers (Irma, Jeannie, and Jane) allowed Mom to help the best she could while they served as back-up.

I had read a bit about Alzheimer's disease, but I was in a "phase" myself of shopping for more information. Long before I learned that Mom had Alzheimer's disease, I had read Nicholas Spark's book entitled *The Notebook,* which later was turned into a movie. I learned more about the disease watching this movie. I had also heard that Mom's friend and confidant had contracted Alzheimer's (the one who was Dad's supervisor) and I was interested in knowing more about the trajectory of the disease. Once I learned of Mom's diagnosis, I read more research articles. My sister had been trying to understand Mom's disease from a distance as she was still living in Florida. She purchased the book entitled *Still Alice* and mailed it to me. In 2015, this book won several Academy Awards! Although it is a story of "early" Alzheimer's which is detected in adults in their 50's or 60's, it provided another lens through which to learn what to expect. In this book, the main character, a university scholar, wrote

herself a letter so that when she got worse, she could remind herself who she had been. That inspired me to write a similar letter to Mom outlining her strengths. I left the letter on her pillow after one visit but I don't know if she was still able to read or if Greg read it to her. Here is the letter.
~~~~~~~~~~~~~

Letter to Mom
July 9, 2009

Dear Mom,
I have been thinking a lot about you recently. I am running through my mind many memories of our childhood, growing up and more recent years. I am thinking about your memory loss and want you to know now how important you are to me and how much I love you. Someday you may not even recognize me and wonder who I am so I want you to have this letter so you will know and remember what a truly amazing life you have led.

I am sharing based on stories you have told me as well as my own memories.
In your early years married to Gordon, you were a multi-tasking wizard. You raised 3 children, played bridge, went to church, gabbed with friends on the phone, joined church circles, and cooked a lot. I loved your spaghetti, fried chicken, homemade pizza, and Eagle brand milk cherry pie.

I also remember:
- o swinging on Lois' front porch swing and her house smelling like eggs and bacon

- ○ when Mr. Wheeler used to smoke out his bees to get the honey
- ○ you locking the screen door with us outside to play (you probably needed a break!)
- ○ the big garden we had in Emory
- ○ You fanning my 3rd degree burn all the way home from Florida
- ○ Me being in the hospital for 21 days and Mrs. Denton's son was the doctor
- ○ Mike biking down the hill on Locust Avenue and you carrying him all the way up
- ○ Playing kick the can until dark. You using a Girl Scout whistle to get us home.

Once we were all in school, you decided to start working part time at the Blacksburg United Methodist church. You job shared with your friend Doris Welch. You typed our school papers on the typewriter there and efficiently compiled everything to print the bulletin each week. Then you worked at the Virginia Tech Bookstore and later for the athletic department and Coach Beamer.

You helped me when I lived in Blacksburg when Whitney was born and I was in graduate school even though you had your own parents to care for. And we had great fun on Ardmore Street having cookouts!

When we moved to Missouri, you came to visit and we went to the Arch in St. Louis and you met all of our friends. Once Ted and I started growing apart, you listened and you helped us both through the deaths of both his parents (1993 and 1994) and Dad (1995). Losing his family was so stressful we decided to move closer to Virginia moving to North Carolina. By now, you were efficiently managing all of the Va Tech coach's playbooks and Coach Beamer's schedule. He didn't know where he was going without consulting with you. You were amazingly efficient and everyone in the athletic offices thought you were great!

Once you met Greg, you both took on many new roles being married, new homes, retirement, and new identities as a couple. Wow! I admire you for working through it and I know it has been tough but your love is strong and will sustain you both. I think one of the most traumatic things for Blacksburg and in your recent years was the shooting on campus. It made everyone feel so unsafe and feel so sorry for the losses of the families. You grieved enough for 10 people for these families.

My kids (Whitney and Shawn) love you so. Someday they will achieve great things but right now, they are trying to find out who they are. I pray everyday that they will discover that soon... but that is all part of life! I know you struggled with accepting Destiny and you didn't think it was a good path for Whitney. But once we both saw that sweet baby and fell in love with her, she won our hearts! Thank-you for praying about how to handle your feelings about that unplanned birth and handling it well with Whitney.

Thank-you for accepting Jack as part of our family. He feels our family warmth and appreciates it.

Mom- you have shown me how to love. You have shown me what a mother's love is about and how to share it with others, how to not be afraid to tell others how I feel and how to be caring and compassionate. You have taught me to be organized and efficient and I am who I am because of so much you have given to me. I love you now and always. Karen
~~~~~~~~~~~~~~~~

The caregivers worked out well for Mom and Greg for about a year. They called me with reports and updates. Mom and Greg were able to keep active by going to the doctors and having visitors from preachers and friends. In 2010, Greg started getting worse and spent time in and out of the hospital. That left Mom alone or else we had to assure that there was a caregiver with her.

In November 2010, Jack and I visited with Mom and Greg. Greg was short of breath and lying in bed (dressed and reading the mail). Jeannie was there. She comes about 8 hours a day and Greg wants her 11-12 hours a day. She seems competent (caring and making meals, picking up and keeping an eye on things including Mom's whereabouts).

I went to Greg's bedside and spoke with him about his recent hospital ordeal. I stayed a few minutes longer to see if there was more he wanted to ask me or share. He told me that Dr. McCoy said he was too weak to continue the cancer treatments that he had just started. His cancer has to do with red blood cells producing oxygen. He had just received nine fresh pints of blood, which should have helped his oxygen level, but he still was short of breath. This was concerning. He said, "you never know what will happen next," and I think he was referring to not making it through the next bout.

I left the room to let him rest then Mom said, "She wants to see you again." I knew what she meant, so I went back to the bedroom to see what Greg wanted. He asked if I was ready to discuss "checking her in somewhere?" I was shocked (inside) but just asked questions. "Why now? What timeline? What parameters? What are you thinking will work?" I needed more information.

He explained that in order to retain and pay the caregivers for overnight stays with Mom, it had cost him $1800 last week. His insurance has not kicked in to help with the payments. He explained that in order for the insurance to pay, he has to be more disabled...like couldn't feed himself or bathe, or shave, etc. Since he could still manage to do those things, his insurance would not pay.

Mom came back in the room and wanted him to come to the table for lunch. Jeannie fixed sandwiches and I asked Greg if I might open up the topic for discussion between Mom, Greg, Jack, and me at the table (Jeannie was in the Living Room). He said (in his most enthusiastic Dr. Gregory way), "I guess."

I said, "Mom, do you want to go home with me for awhile?" I was figuring that I would need time to work out arrangements. She said, "No, I am not leaving him." I offered, "Well his insurance won't pay for Jeannie and in order for you to stay here at home alone, we need to get into your resources (and bank account) to pay for her to stay here with you both. Otherwise you must go home with me or we need to find a nice new place for you to live." She said, "Then I will pay from my accounts." I asked Greg if I had power of attorney or any ability to sign her checks. He said that he didn't think so. Mom started getting out bank statements and folders asking if these would help. I tried to piece together how much money she had. She brought out her purse and asked if there was anything in there that would be useful.

That afternoon, we all made a trip to her two banks. Mom signed the forms that made me a joint owner on her account. I started out as a co-owner on the accounts and as Power of Attorney, only at her death. Power of Attorney seemed too complicated at this point (to resolve in an afternoon). Greg sat there and watched.

It became more and more evident that Greg was getting sicker and that Mom was not getting any smarter. In March, I wrote her a poem for her birthday with photos of me and of mom pasted all around the poem. In May, she mailed it to Sherry and told her Happy Birthday from her. Gee!! We received strange things in the mail from her. Once I got a list of her things that would be willed to each of us. Mike got two copies of the same thing and Sherry got an empty envelope!

My best friend from childhood came to visit me and wanted to see Mom. Mom used to adore Krista and visa versa. Mom showed Krista around the condo then paused on the stairs and asked, "Now, how do I know you?" Krista patiently explained about us being childhood friends. When Krista was out of sight, Mom said, "I don't know her, but I feel like I love her!"

It was shortly after that I agreed to arrange a meeting to tell Mom that she would be moving to Wheatland Hills Assisted Living in Christiansburg, VA. I went to visit her while Greg was in the hospital. Here is my email after that visit.
~~~~~~~~~~
From Karen to Mike & Sherry
Sent: Thursday, June 16, 2011 5:46 PM
Subject: Mom

Hey-
We spent the night with Mom last night. I literally slept in her bed but she slept like a log. Greg was at the hospital getting blood and is still there hopefully to come home tonight. While there, his doctor and a social worker talked with him about the fact that the yet unexplained respiratory issue could be stress-related as he is worried about Mom, his death, dying, and her well-being.

Greg's son, John called me this afternoon to approach the subject of her moving on into

Wheatland Hills. I called WH and they have potential space for her if we move fast. They require her to get a physical within 30 days prior to her admittance and $500 deposit. They have a deal called "respite" that could allow her to move in for 2 months or less and leave again if we chose. The difficult part is approaching her about this. Sunday I have arranged a meeting at their condo. Greg should be out of the hospital by then. His son, John will join Jack and me as will Jeannie and Reggie, the preacher. We will sit down with her @ 3:00 to have this difficult discussion. I would like to approach it in a positive way saying that there will be food, activities and friends there! I will make it clear that Greg will visit her daily when he can.

I suppose we can put this off and wait until he dies or go ahead and get her settled now. I am thinking of proposing July 2 as a move in date. We would need to pack her familiar things, etc. and get the physical.

We may need Shawn or Garrett to come help with the moving of a few of her things (chair, bedding, clothing, coffee table, etc.) There is a twin bed already there in the room. I just wanted to keep you up to date. Karen

~~~~~~~~~~

When we convened the meeting. Rev. Tuck and Greg's son John joined Jack and me. We talked with Mom and Greg. Greg sat silently rather tearful from time to time. Rev. Reggie reasoned with Mom (which is not easy with a person who has memory issues). She said she "would not go and would not leave Greg." We tabled the discussion but felt at least we had planted the seed.

The next week, I asked Amanda, the memory care coordinator at Wheatland, to come to assess her to see if she was eligible for memory care. Greg told her to show Amanda around the condo. She did. Once they were upstairs, Mom opened the closet with all of her clothes and said, " And this is where I do all of my cooking." We figured she was a shoe in at that time - and she was!

Chapter 6
Wheatland Hills

On July 1, 2012, we activated our move-in plan for
Mom to live at Wheatland Hills. After two weeks,
she had now forgotten our conversation. Marge was
to come pick her up to take her to have her hair cut
at 9:00 am while Mike, Lisa, Jack and I were to come
select the things she would need to take to
Wheatland. The in-home caregivers knew what was
to come, as did Greg. We brought our truck and
Mike was to bring a flat bed trailer for loading. We
knew we were all to work very fast. Timing was
critical. When Mom was away from home, she
would often say "take me home now" or "why are
we doing this?" So we knew she would become
irritated if she were away too long. We had to be
ready.

All went according to plan FOR THE MOST part. First
she didn't want to get into the car with Marge for
her hair appointment. Greg ended up taking her to
the beauty shop. Afterwards, Marge and her
husband Travis were to take her back to their house
for coffee to kill some more time so we could pack.
At the condo, we got busy. I put sticky notes on
what was to go on the truck and what was to go on
the trailer. Some items went in my vehicle to come
home with me. Some items were to go to the
Goodwill Community Foundation, and others were
going to Wheatland. I was trying to mentally
categorize things as to who got what while still
preserving and packing what she needed. We had 6
people and approximately 2 hours to complete the
move. I busied myself barking orders to people right

and left. Everyone had a job. About that time, Greg arrived back home and exploded saying, "You are not coming in here and ransacking my home." Everyone froze and looked at me. I stopped and calmly pulled him aside saying, "I know this is stressful for everyone involved. We will not take anything that does not belong to Mom. As you know, we have limited time and we need to act quickly." He said, "well, ok then." So we went back to work.

I asked Greg which TV to pack. Once designated, Jack started disassembling the cords and packing them up. Greg stopped him midway, deciding he needed to keep the power strip and we were not to take it. I needed a little rug for the bathroom. I held up one from the hallway and he said, "No, you better buy her another rug. Not that one." And so the morning went. By 10:00, we were loaded and on our way to Wheatland. By 10:30, Marge and Travis were calling saying that Mom was restless and ready to go home. I asked Travis to "buy me at least 30 more minutes." In her new quarters, we propped up photos of the children, arranged trinkets, and hung pictures on the walls. I hung up her clothing and put her shoes on a rack. Mike and I left at 11:00 to go back to the condo to get Mom. We left Lisa and Jack to complete the settling of the new room.

As Lisa and Jack worked in Mom's new room, many of the residents started wandering in and out. A woman wandered into Mom's room and started messing with her things. Lisa told her "this is not your room." She kept pilfering and said, "I just need one." Finally Lisa pulled off a paper towel to give her and the resident left happy with that ONE paper towel. Oh, boy this is gonna' be a fun bunch of neighbor-residents!

When Mike and I got to Mom's condo, we sat in the car a moment, took a breath and I said a prayer out loud to God asking for guidance in what we needed to do. Mike, a lifetime firefighter, had an ambulance on call in case it came to some sort of restraint, God forbid! We walked in the front door and Jeannie, the caregiver, just rolled her eyes and shook her head (not good). Mom was looking for something that she said was "missing." It was the TV. She was wandering around asking Jeannie where it was and Jeannie replied, "Honey, I just don't know."

Making herself look busy, Jeannie was fixing sandwiches in the kitchen and called Greg to lunch. He scampered to the kitchen like a bunny, scared to be in the middle of what was to come. Mom asked where he was going all of a sudden. I took Mom by the arm and told her, "I know where your things are." Further," I said, "Mike and I are here to take care of you and take you somewhere that you will like."

She said she wasn't leaving Greg. But then she said, "I hate that woman in the kitchen!" I reminded her that she had told me years ago that this is what she wanted (to go to a "home"). I said, "Today is the day that we are going to move to the new place. Remember we talked about it." She said, "I am not going anywhere and that woman in the kitchen is a bitch." I saw this as the opportunity I needed and said, "Really? Are they not being nice to you?" She said no they were not. I said, "then let's go somewhere where they are nice to you. Come with me. " She asked if that "bitch will be gone when I get back?" I replied, "You don't have to see her any more." I asked her to go get her purse and come get in the car with me, which she did. Thank you Lord!!

Mike widened his eyes (in a high five kind of way) and followed us in his truck back to Wheatland. I drove Mom in her own car to Wheatland. She started crying a bit and said, " This is the end. It is over." I didn't think that it was a suicidal statement but as the day went on what it seemed she was implying is that Greg would never come see her and she said, " I guess I don't have a husband any more. " It made wonder me what he had told her. She said, "You'll see. He won't come out here."

We walked into the doors of Wheatland at 11:30. Phew! The process had taken 2.5 hours. Jack and Lisa had put on the final settling touches. When we arrived and she looked at the familiar things in her room, she commented, "That's a nice picture of Mother and Daddy." We pointed out other familiar things and told her this was her new home. She liked it. Thank you, Lord, again!

Getting Settled in Memory Care – Day 1
Mike and Jack went with Mom to lunch, and met a few of the residents and staff. Everyone at Wheatland was welcoming and wonderful. While Jack and Mike ate lunch with Mom, I went to sign the caregiving contracts. Lisa guarded the room in case the woman who wanted "just one" came back. We recognized one of the residents. It was Mrs.

Beamer, who had been our elementary school principal. She was also the aunt to football coach Frank Beamer, whom Mom worked for before retiring. We greeted Mrs. Beamer and she was as pleasant as ever.

During lunch, Jack, Mom, and Mike were eating when a woman in a wheelchair who at first appeared non-responsive, suddenly sat bolt upright in her wheelchair, looked straight at Jack and said, "Shut up! You get outa here and never come back." Unsure what prompted that, Mike and Jack just exchanged looks, shook their heads and kept calm for Mom!

There were many funny stories along the way as we met others in the memory care wing! The woman who wanted "just one" was named Betty. She kept coming back in because se seemed to like our dog, Kramer that we brought as a calming influence for Mom. Betty would just walk right in to pet Kramer. Not mincing words, Jack finally quietly said, "Go away Betty!"

Lisa and I left Wheatland to go back to get another small table we needed at the House. Greg had Jeannie already were packing up Mom's knick-knacks in boxes. I asked him if he was coming to see her and he said, "I don't know." Now I was really wondering what he was thinking. Did he just feel he had just dumped her? When we got back to Mom again, I called on my cell phone to tell Greg her

phone wasn't working yet. He asked to talk with her. I am not sure what was said but he implied he would be visiting that day.

Throughout the move-in day, I felt the prayers of others. I prayed with my brother before we went in to get Mom. Jack sat with her at lunch table and said a blessing. God was truly holding us through this! The move went so much better than it could have.

As the weeks passed, Mom got nicely settled and made friends. I had made her a pictorial chart of what to do each day like teeth brushing and dressing. I don't know that she ever looked at it but it seemed a good idea at the time.

In my research about Alzheimer's, I had read that the spouse without the disease begins to feel a bit like an outsider. I was glad I had that knowledge when Greg questioned, "Why are the men and women on the same hallway?" I told him it wasn't a dorm and that they are certainly all adults. There were only 2 men. One, Mr. Surface, was married and his wife lived on the hallway too. He was quite a flirt, but he always had a handshake and smile. The other was Dr. C. He had been a university administrator so with a common interest in higher education they seated Mom with him. They quickly became friends, which really angered Greg. Greg started locking mom's door and asking the staff to serve her dinner in her room. He would have a caregiver come pick Mom up and bring Mom back to the house for most of the day, then eat dinner with her in Wheatland to protect her from making more friends. He asked that staff seat Mom back to back from Mr. C. so they could not see each other. I felt as if the man was harmless and that Greg was over reacting. Greg continued to pick her up each day and take her back to the condo. One day she was straightening a banner hanging by their condo garage and somehow she fell and broke her arm. Oh great! We are paying

 big bucks for good care and now she has a broken arm.

We had a phone installed in her room and we called her regularly. We had cable installed so Mom and

Greg could watch television together. One weekend, four months after her move-in, all of the children and grand children went to visit. What a fun day that was. Sherry even came from Florida to see Mom's new residence. By then Greg was using a cane and was very short of breath. After the family visit, everyone spent the weekend going through Grandmommy's things to see if they could use any of them. Everything smelled like Mom and her hint of Jean Nate' bath splash! Sherry asked me to store the things she had selected until she could retire and move back to Virginia. Mike said he didn't want any of the things but then took a few select items.

The conflict between Greg and Dr. C began to build.

By now, Jack and I had our house on the market in Raleigh. We were traveling back and forth constructing the hangar. One evening, I got a call that Mom was in the Emergency Room and that Greg had taken her at 9:30pm. Her stomach was hurting. I called Wheatland to get the rest of the story and learned they had just given her nausea medication and sent her home. Apparently Mike had witnessed her being upset during his visit the day before. We learned that she told staff that she and Greg had disagreement. Then Greg had insisted on taking her to the ER.

As I learned more background, it seemed that the stress with Dr. C had escalated. Dr C. was a black man and mom was becoming attached to him. They had been sitting together at lunch most days. One day, a black woman joined him for lunch. That was the day that sent mom into an unexplainable tizzy (perhaps jealousy?). Mike and Lisa stopped in for a visit and smoothed things over but I guess the feelings lingered and upset her somehow. Who knows what was going on in that slipping brain? Or in Greg's!

I started reading Pauline Boss' book called *"Loving Someone with Dementia."* Her primary point is that with Alzheimer's or Dementia, the caregiver (any one of us plus Greg) must reconstruct a new perception of their relationship with the demented person. She would never be the Mom (wife) we knew again and although we could mourn over that loss or her life or what we imagined in her waning years, she would never be the same. Convincing Greg of this was a real task as well.

However, we had to think dually to not only recall those past memories of Mom but also to construct a new Mom/Margaret and "get into that space with her." She had new friends and new short-term memories at Wheatland.

One woman in the P. Boss book shared that her husband, John, was in a facility where another resident calls "John her boyfriend." The woman feels on the outside but has learned to incorporate the new friend into their life as well now. I am afraid that was not what Greg was doing with Mr. C. Instead we thought he may have been scolding her like a child (Mom never took well to that) and it upset her physically and emotionally. My guess was that was what happened when Greg took her to the ER. Greg was highly jealous and although I would have liked him to read the Boss book and change, I knew that was not going to happen.

Caring for a parent from a distance can be really hard. Sherry didn't have the luxury of seeing Mom when she wanted to since as a school principal, working an 11-month school schedule. This email depicts her feelings:

~~~~~
From Sherry to Mike & Karen
I called her yesterday and hung up crying. I asked if she had gotten a stuffed Halloween kitty I sent, she said yes and then said her feet were bleeding and all covered with clothes. Then said I can't tell you how, he is coming to get me and then was ready to hang up . . .I am almost scared to call any more, wonder if she is as traumatized by my calling as I am by her answering? Poor Mom.
~~~~~

 At Christmas, I took Mom shopping so she would have something to give to Greg. She had fun watching the gifts be wrapped. We sang *Silent Night* and *Santa Claus is Coming to Town* together in the car.

After six months (January 2012) at Wheatland, I was asked to come in for a planning meeting. It is protocol to meet with the family and be sure things are going ok. I asked Greg and Mom both to join me. I felt I needed to bring up the issue of Dr. C in Amanda's presence to see if we might resolve anything since Greg was still angry with him and Mom seemed to like him. We had the meeting and at the end, Amanda asked if there was anything else we wanted to discuss. I looked at Greg who, looked as if he had steam coming out his ears. He said, "I better not say something I will regret." But then he exploded! He stood up and slammed his fist on the table saying, "They are trying to turn her into a nigga whore." I hate even writing that on paper but the shock value on paper is nothing like the shock value of hearing it.

Being in the field of human development, I have learned how to listen and diffuse emotions. In my super calm voice, I said, "First of all you sound racist, which we won't be able to resolve here, and secondly you sound angry." He sat down. Amanda and I stuck to the arrangements of seating them back-to-back and let Greg vent. He explained that he feared losing her and my guess is he was really speaking of his own imminent demise. He went on to say that they go everywhere together and he was afraid that would change. I heard the pain in his voice beyond his words. Shocking still -but sad!

When we called Mom on the phone, she would say she was waiting for "him" or "my husband." She really had forgotten his name and ours. By February, Greg contracted a blood clot in his leg that caused him to be in the hospital for a few days. Once released, he went home and started taking blood thinners. The caregivers continued even while he was hospitalized. As soon as he got out of the hospital, Jeannie drove him to pick up Mom. I happened to be leaving Wheatland as they arrived and followed them out of the parking lot. Jeannie chauffeured while Mom and Greg sat in the back seat as if they were on a date. I watched them kiss and touch until I had to turn to go a different direction.

He couldn't have been out of the hospital for more than a week when he woke up with a bleeding nose. The caregiver du jour, Jane, called 911 and again he was taken to the hospital. They packed his nose but because of the blood clot could not discontinue the blood thinners.

When I called, Mom asked where "he" was and I told her that "he" was sick and once out of the hospital I was sure he would come to see her. I called about every other day to check on Greg. He was in the hospital for about 2 weeks before contracting the highly contagious disease of MRSA. I was told that he called out for Margaret to "get him out of there." He also called out for his first wife, Charlotte.

Greg's son, John, asked if Wheatland would allow Mom to come visit. Due to the contagion, they were very careful and cautious before finally allowing her to go provided she was masked and robed. Mike and Lisa took her to see Greg where she talked to him and kissed his non-responsive brow. The next day, Greg let go and was gone.

Chapter 7
Life After Greg

Mike and I felt as if we should tell Mom in person that Greg had died. Sherry offered to come in from Florida, but as a school principal, she had more difficulty getting away and we felt we could handle it. Jack had recently had a little run in with a garage door spring and had stitches in his hand, so he could not fly me in his the plane. A good friend and Jack's flying instructor from Raleigh flew me to Blacksburg to meet Mike to go to Wheatland to tell Mom. She ranted, cried, kicked up her feet and was at a loss. To change the mood and scenery, we took her out to dinner where she settled down. To allow Greg's four sons to be present for the funeral, the service was delayed a week. In that time, I shopped for appropriate clothing for Mom and Mike and I again strategized how to handle the visitation and funeral with her.

Marvelously, Mike and Lisa visited her that week to check on her status. By this time, they had moved full time into their new home in to Floyd, VA, which is about 30 minutes from Christiansburg. They became the bridge between the death and time for the funeral. Mike sent updates to us when the visited. I am so thankful that my brother, the big burley firefighter, is such a loving part of this family and that Lisa encourages his involvement!
~~~~~~~~~

Mike's update to the family
We had an interesting visit with Mom today, in brief, taking her out to lunch and then some shopping. That really helped her attitude. She

kept repeating "thank you so much for getting me out of there, otherwise I would have gone crazy." We had her out for about two hours and that was about all she wanted. I'm beginning to realize every day is different with her. I think we try to normalize our relationships and experiences especially with family. I think that is no longer an option with Mom. Every experience with her is dynamic. Some things are unexpected...we must get used to it.

At lunch at the Texas Roadhouse I was sitting next to her talking about the predicted snow tomorrow and she said to me "will you just shut up? You're scaring me!" I know I'm loud but I quickly realized that I needed to adjust myself around her. Frankly my feelings were hurt a just wee bit, but I shook it off and she was quickly back to kissing me and telling me "I love you too."

At first today she was weeping and saying her usual, "he's gone honey, he's gone". I'm not sure who "honey" is, I'm pretty sure it's not Lisa or me, I think oddly it's Greg! After many "where is he's?" somehow I popped out, "Mom, Jesus had a toothache and Greg is tending to Jesus' teeth!" At which she smiled, and even giggled. Finally something positive I thought. I asked Mom if we could just agree to say that Greg is just working on Jesus' teeth, and surprisingly she agreed. So, whenever she said, "Where is he?" I would reply, "Greg is working on Jesus' teeth," which seemed to placate and even please her.

After lunch she somehow communicated the fact

that she had no chewing gum, so we stopped at a CVS and Lisa bought her four huge packages of gum and a couple of chocolate wafer bars which pleased Mom immensely.

She is very sensitive about her remote control that she hides in the cushion of her chair. She would not let us change the TV from the History Channel. It is certain she would never find that channel again. She has a CD player in the room but she wants nothing of it.

In all, Mom is grieving in a healthy way. I think she is slowly starting to deal with it all. I'm sure the funeral next week will reignite any and all feelings she's having today, but I think she'll come out of all this with time. Remember, every visit is different. It would be odd if any two experiences with her were ever the same anymore; I could be making erroneous predictions for sure. When we left she was ready to be back in her room and her mood was markedly better. The visit and mini-trip was quite successful and Lisa and I left there almost mentally exhausted (our minds are learning and adapting so much so fast it's like being in college again). But we felt like we made a difference in her life for the better and that felt good.

~~~~~~~

The week of the funeral, Jack and I drove from North Carolina and stayed in Floyd with Mike and Lisa but drove over early to Christiansburg to prepare Mom for the funeral. I had purchased a new black jacket with a brightly color scarf. The preparation for the funeral home visitation was somewhat rocky. When I arrived with the clothing and told her we were going to see Greg in the casket and visit with the friends who would come pay their respects, she said, "I don't do that anymore. I am not going." She was none too pleasant and definitely didn't want to go.

Finally she gave in and said, "What do you want me to do?" I said, "I would like to wash your hair, brush your teeth, and put on these lovely clothes." She stood in the tub and said "in here?" I said, "Sure" as I tried to let her take the lead. She said, "But I have my clothes on!" So instead of a full shower, I asked her to just bend over the sink and I would wash her hair. She cried the whole time. I took the blow dryer to style her hair, all the while she was telling me that I was "killin her" and to "just leave!" I gently worked with her, combed her hair, told her how nice she looked. Luckily a nurse assistant came in to help. I said, "Since she about hates me now, can you help her finish dressing?" The assistant did a masterful job. I kept handing her things (a broach, earrings, a

scarf, black jacket) though the bathroom door until she was dressed. By the time Mike arrived, she was ready. Phew!

Once at the funeral home, she saw Greg in the casket and started to back away. I told her she didn't have to go in and we could leave after she saw the family. But in the strength of the Clamon blood, she walked up to the casket, kissed and petted him and stalwartly greeted at least 100 people who visited. At one point she asked me to take a picture of him. I went to my car to retrieve my i-pad and did as I was asked. Jack was ever so embarrassed with this. However, I do recall Mom taking photos of Grandmother and Bookey in their caskets so I guess this is just a family behavior! We stayed close by Mom and after about an hour and a half, she was ready to go. I was so proud she pulled herself together for the visitation!

On the day of the funeral, I again helped Mom get ready and this time there was no fight. When Mike arrived, he had printed the photo of "dead Greg" and gave it to Mom. I was sort of hoping to not to give it to her until she asked for it but Mike and I got our communication wires crossed on that one. We left the photo in the room and went on to the funeral. It went smoothly and she accepted it gracefully. The Methodist women prepared a family lunch after the graveside funeral for the family. Everyone commented how well Mom had done. The next week, Mike and Lisa faithfully traveled to see Mom. Here is his report:

~~~~~~

In an effort to continue with Mom's, post Greg rehab, Lisa and I rolled over the mountain to C-Burg again today to take her out for lunch, and some activities. She was ready to get out of her room and was very grateful that we came to get her. She has oddly placed Greg's moribund casket photo center stage in her room.

We then went to the duck pond at Tech and fed the ducks and geese (again), which was fun, then to downtown B-Burg for lunch and then to Pier 1 for some shopping. Between Mom and me our patience ran out after about 15 minutes and she was ready to head back to her room. We sat around there for a bit watching The History Channel (as usual, she won't let anyone touch her remote to change the channels) and then Lisa and I exited to head to The Home Depot for some things we needed for the house. All in all it was a good visit, about 2.5 hours, just about a new record except for the funeral. She seemed to have a good time and really appreciated getting out of her room.

During our time with her, she conveyed that she thinks someone is trying to get into her room to swipe things and sleep in her bed. We discussed this with WL (Wheatland) management and they said it was probably her imagination but they would keep an extra eye on anyone entering her usually locked room. Her pillow was normal, her hair was washed and her breath was better than usual. Amanda (lead memory care person) understood our concerns with her breath, which was punctuated by Karen's email yesterday about the tooth brushing.

I think we will start weaning her from everyday visits, which we can't sustain indefinitely. I can't over emphasize to my family what an asset Lisa has been to this whole dramatic and dynamic process. She continues to monitor Mom with more acuity than I could ever have. She intuitively knows what Mom thinks, and how to order her food. She is infinitely sensitive to Mom's needs and has the energy to give something extra; I am continually amazed at her tenacity. I guess we'll continue this saga day-to-day. Each visit is mentally exhausting just trying to fill in the gaps and anticipating Mom's needs. She'll probably live for many more years, at this rate so we can use all the help we can get. Our latest goal is to bring her to Floyd and hang a few hours at the house before returning her to WL; we're building to that end. In conclusion, as strange as it seems, Lisa and I both think we detect a teensy improvement in her cognitive function...maybe just wishful thinking, but we think she is handling Greg's death and somehow learning to enjoy life w/o "him." Well, that's today's report. Love to all of our family.

~~~~~~

About this time, Jack and I were busily trying to sell our North Carolina house to move to Virginia and build our Bed & Breakfast home at Smith Mountain Lake. We were ever so appreciative of Mike and Lisa who did the lion's share of Mom monitoring after Greg's death. We had heard that Mom was sleeping with the "dead Greg" photo. I told Marge about it and the next time she visited, she located the photo and while Mom wasn't looking, hid it behind some other photos out of sight. Mike continued to send updates.

Mike's update to the family March 12, 2012

We left Mom alone over the weekend, last visit was Friday, and ventured over today to get her out of that room again. It was a nice warm, sun shiny, spring-like day. It was probably our best day ever with her. We actually think we see documentable improvements in her cognitive ability!!! I'll use bullets today:

- We all (mostly me) have got to remember that the first 5 or 10 minutes of arriving in her room are "the absolute refractory period." When we (I) arrive it's like a three ring circus shows up. She goes from dullness and staring at the TV to commotion and noise. She needs some time to ramp up to this. Today I marched slower than normal, and quieter, and then decided all of her clocks and watch need to be set a hour ahead, from Sunday. This about blew her mind and I had to backtrack resetting her (4) clocks throughout the afternoon. Damn I'm slow!
- We decided first today to drive by our old house on Locust. Not sure how she would react, we set out through the neighborhood. I pointed out several houses that were some of our old friends. Some she acted like she remembered, some she admitted that she didn't. Then we turned onto the "dip",

which I think she truly remembered. (Note that the "dip" is a huge 25% grade in the road entering our neighborhood) And as we turned onto Locust, she asked me to slow down so she could look closer at the houses and low and behold, she knew exactly which house was ours!! We stopped in front and talked about old times.

- Then off to the duck pond again. I drove right through campus, which took about 15 minutes with all the students back, crossing the streets. But she just loves the campus and points out the streets she would drive on and buildings she remembered.
- Lunch was at a place called Lefty's. The French fries were a hit, but not the sandwich. Live and learn. I had to take a phone call and left Mom with Lisa. Lisa said she mentioned that her (Mom's) birthday was next week and both her daughters would be here. She said something to the effect of "don't bring them all to my house", which Lisa thought (like I mentioned above) that too many people in her room is overwhelming. Lisa said the girls could head to the park (picnic) and we would pick her up and take her over. That seemed fine to her.
- Back to WH. She knows where the turn is off of 460 to WH and points it out. We told her if the weather was good Thursday, we would probably come get her and bring her to Floyd. She says she wants to see our house and seemed excited. Amanda said that "Mrs. Gregory" actually

participated in some exercise this morning and they had a therapy dog drop in and she really enjoyed that. Lisa asked Amanda if anyone had seen her about her cough, which was worse today. Amanda was going to follow up with Becky (the resident nurse).

- Eventfully, Mom didn't mention "Him" (Dead Greg) for the first time since he died! This was wonderful for us not to have to hear her incantations about "him" over and over. Also the Dead Greg photo that Albert Einstein (Karen) took and Marge skillfully removed (thank God) remains in hiding and Mom doesn't seem to miss it.

So the visit was more positive than negative for once, AND taking Mom out of that room is inherently healthy for her. She is repeatedly thankful and seems more secure and less nervous upon every visit...this we feel, is positive.

March 22nd was Mom's birthday. Lisa had the good idea to have a picnic at the Town Caboose Park. Sherry and John came to town and met with a builder who will start to build their house, also at Smith Mountain Lake. It was grand to have all us kids together for Mom's birthday. We had party hats, gifts and cake. We took a walk and Mom

was child like. We all had a festive time. I so love this photo of Mike and Mom walking together and used it for the cover of this little book.

The next week, Sherry called Mom to tell her what a good visit it was and what fun we had on her birthday. Mom said, "We didn't do that." Oh, well. Poor Sherry – the trials of caregiving from a distance!

The next month, I called mom on the phone. Here is how the conversation went:

Mom: Hello

Me: Hey mom. Whatcha doin?

Mom: Just waiting to eat again

Me: I wanted to tell you that we sold our house. We will move closer to you and live in Virginia

Mom: You will like that

Me: yes we will live closer to you

Mom: That's a long way away (changing subject)

Me: I saw a picture that Amanda sent of you stirring up some sugar cookies.

Mom: I didn't do that.

Me: Remember stirring up the egg in a bowl?

Mom: That was somebody else, I didn't do that.

(changing subject again)
M: It is a pretty day. You could walk outside.
Mom: No I don't do that
Me: Sure you could. I will take you outside when
I come visit.
Mom: I don't want to do that.
Me: well I love ya, I will call you again sometime.
Mom: ok. I love you too.
~~~~~~~~~~~~

In May when I visited, Mom was sitting in the
Wheatland courtyard with other residents blowing
bubbles. She had on 2 shirts and a velour jacket and
it was about 100 degrees. She got up as Kramer (my
little dog) and I approached and we went inside. She
had her remote with her, which I convinced her to
leave in her room. I noted her breath was
horrendous! Before taking her out, I had her brush
her teeth!

We went to Panera Bread and sat outside since we
had Kramer. We split a sandwich and I got her a
peach smoothie. She went with me to pick up some
reclaimed wood I hope to use in decorating. She
sang to Kramer and told him over and over how she
loved him. Her clothes looked to have a bit of feces
on the front so I had her change.
That confused her. I took the clothes to wash. She
walked me to the door and waved goodbye.

The following months, it seemed that her behavior
became less predictable. Anytime there was a
stressful event, it seems that she deteriorated and
this time, the death of Greg seemed to be adding to
her agitated behavior. In June, firstborn grandson
Tony visited from Colorado. This was his insightful

family update about Mom from Tony.

~~~~~~~~~~

From Nephew Tony:
Now let me say this up front. I had spoken to myself, then voiced this thought out loud to Mike on the way over indicating that I really appreciate everyone's concern about me seeing her. You know the state she's in and I appreciate everyone looking out. Secondly, I believed it to be harder on all of us than it is for Grandmommy. For her, she's living a complete "Be Here Now" existence, meaning all she knows is to live by the second hand. So with that in mind, I prepped myself for my visit.

When we got to her room, the door was locked. Lisa found a nurse who informed us that she said she did not wish to eat lunch and that was she was in bed.   The nurse unlocked her door and we slowly walked in to a darkened room with the lights off and the shades drawn closed. Mike announced we were there as we walked in towards the bed. Grandmommy was under the covers, in her PJs, and was most certainly awakened by our entering the room.   Mike and I sat on couch as Mike spoke with her and asked if she wanted to go out for shopping or ice cream.   Grandmommy's response was something like, "Well I can do that" or perhaps it was "Well if you want me to."

She was lethargic … groggy … very much out of it … like a child who was woken up in the middle of the night, except that it was 1:30 PM.   Her immediate thought upon getting out of bed was that she did not know what to wear, and did not know the next step in getting dressed and prepared for leaving her room. Mike and I left her room and Lisa started to dig in the closet for something to wear.

As Mike and I were in the hallway, he asked a couple of the nurses why they would allow her to be in bed at 1:30 PM. The nurses said that due to the full moon the night before that everyone's cycles were slightly off.

Lisa and Grandmommy walked out of the room and she instantly hugged on Mike, then set her eyes on me and told me how cute I was. We then hugged and kissed as I took her hand and held it as we walked down the hallway. She said "I didn't think I could still do this" while walking, still very groggy and quietly lamenting how tired she was and how she was awoken. I promised her the sun would help, and that was probably solar powered like myself.

We hopped in my little rental car and headed up a few blocks to a Cold Stone Creamery where we all enjoyed a cup of ice cream. By the time we reached Cold Stone, she was 180 degrees different. She stepped over a parking spot curb as I told her she danced over it, which incited a little jig she busted into ... Mike had mentioned how when she's in a good mood she will dance a little bit and sing a little song. Over our desert course at Cold Stone she broke in to a few songs and a few little dance moves.

She was very sweet and very kind and kept telling me how cute I was and how much she liked me. I would come back with compliments to her about her hair and earrings and shoes, which made her giggle. She also asked a few times where the money was ...

It was little comments like that that I found slightly amusing. You would say something to her and without missing a beat she would answer with something completely disjointed and disconnected, like "well that's how I got there." It reminded me of t-shirts from japan with broken English that have a stream of words to it but they do not connect properly with each other.

I remember when this disease first began; she had problems remembering nouns ... It's progressed to the point where she just doesn't remember, period. But as much as she does not remember memories, she still knows English, she can still speak, she can still say thank you when you hold the door open for her, she guided us back to Wheatland from the ice cream shop and seemed to know where to turn. She recognizes colors. She knew you were not supposed to turn on a red light although she did not know what it was called.

When we got back to Wheatland, Harry was in the hallway sitting in a chair. This is newly labeled "boyfriend" Grandmommy has been hanging out with. Harry's wife apparently died some years ago and Harry has some memory care needs as well. Grandmommy gave him a kiss on the lips and we left for her room. She turned on the TV when we got back, but no one could find the remote control ...she hides the remote, but of course can never remember where she put it.

Accepting the fact that Grandmommy's memory is severely deteriorated is way tough on all of us. I now realize she cannot remember things, she's not be able to read, not be able to remember anyone's names, and apparently not even able to remember activities from day to day. Mike says she wouldn't even remember if someone was to come back the day after a visit that they were even there the day before ... but she's so kind, so sweet, she will tell you she loves you, and she likes you over and over and over again.

It's very much like she has reverted to being a child. It's tough on us because we have memories we cannot share, nor relive, nor talk about, but for her, she is simply living in the now, living in the moment. She seems content, and pleasantly happy, and so kind and loving.

Mike told me the tales of not understanding why Greg did not visit her when he was sick. Then Mike mentioned how he took her to the hospital to see Greg, and if that made sense to her why he could not visit. Mike said that last visit was two days before he passed away, and when they had to break the news to her, she had a deep hard cry. Of course, thinking of her losing him, and Greg losing his own life, I was deeply saddened. Then hearing how it was much harder on her when they told her that she had to leave the house and move in to Wheatland, and that made me sad too for it was truly a mark of an end of a chapter of her life, of all of our lives, and how precious life and family really is.

Dear Family, I know we do not always have the

time to visit with each other as often as we would like, but I love you all very much. We are family. As a teenager it was easy to forget that as we grow up selfish and self-centered and the family thing just doesn't matter as much, and now as I have reached 40, I realize that family is amongst the most important of life's values and riches and how much I treasure and adore you all.

(End of Tony's email)

~~~~~~~~~~~

After moving to Virginia, I visited Mom more often. Whenever I tried to call her on the phone to tell her I wanted to come, she never answered the phone. My guess is she was sitting there wondering where that ringing noise was coming from! And, she had begun to spend more time on the common area with Harry. One day Jack and I went by to see her. She wanted to sit in the common area near Harry, her newly proclaimed "husband." I wanted to divert her a bit from Harry. The Ellen Show was on television in the common area. During Ellen's opening dance

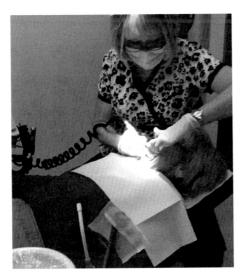

extravaganza, I had Mom dance with me. That was a fun moment!

We had noticed that her breath was (still) atrocious so I made a dental appointment to have her teeth cleaned. We went to Greg's old dental practice and they all knew her there. The hygienist said that she must brush at least once a day if not 3 times a day or she will get gum disease or lose her teeth.

When we were returned from the dentist, Mom said she hated "him" and looked really angry. I asked who she hated and she said, "my husband." It was Harry. While there, I ran into Harry's daughter Suzie, whom I had gone to high school with. I jokingly told her that I guess we are now sister's in law. She didn't really find that amusing. She conveyed that once she had been sitting with Mom and Harry. She said that Mom told Harry, "I wish I had never married you." Harry replied, "I don't remember asking you!" And so it goes. I had a report that Mom got angry with Harry and threw her wedding ring and diamond ring across the grassy courtyard in anger. They were her wedding rings from her marriage to Greg. The rings were never found. I can imagine one of the dedicated staff members found them to be quite valuable pieces!

The following week, I had my 7-year old grand daughter visiting. Mom loved being with Destiny and Destiny very carefully would take Mom's hand and lead her around. On this day, we had two important stops to make. Mom had a neurologist appointment and I needed to go by the attorney's office in Blacksburg to deliver a Power of Attorney (POA) for the sale of the Condo on behalf of Mom. We had a nice visit during our drive to Salem to the doctor. Dr. H adjusted her meds since I had received some calls about Mom's agitation, including the time that she had hit Harry on the back of the head and knocked his glasses off.

When we returned from the doctor's office, we seated Mom in the lunchroom. Another resident approached Destiny. Over and over the woman was saying something incomprehensible that sounded like "Ham, ham, hm, hm, ham ham, etc." The nurse said the resident wanted to kiss Destiny. Destiny allowed it—both cheeks! When we left, Destiny said, "I can't get that woman out of my head!"

While in town, Destiny and I dropped in to see an attorney to straighten out the Power of Attorney so that I was allowed to sign papers for Mom. The attorney said that I needed an original POA in order to close the real estate sale of their condo. He drew up a new POA and I backtracked to Wheatland to see if Mom might be able to sign the document. I asked Destiny to sit in the chair behind me since the same

"Ham, hm, Ham" woman was roaming the halls. I gathered 2 (staff) witnesses and a notary around Mom as she wrote "Marg" but then the rest of the signature deteriorated. That little bit of signature, however was enough to be notarized and witnessed. As I turned to leave, I noticed my precious little Destiny sitting in the chair with huge tears rolling down her sweet face as she stared at the "Ham, Hm" woman.

Shortly after that visit, the incident phone calls started increasing from the Wheatland Hills staff. The staff reported that Mom had tripped Harry. I heard later that his family had to take him to the ER for a shoulder x-ray. I don't think my newly appointed sister-in-law was too happy about this arrangement and I was quite embarrassed! The next call, reported that Mom had knocked on his door and when he opened it, she kicked him. However, each time the staff would try to separate Mom from Harry, she pitched a fit. I felt like I was the parent and Mom was the child in day care. During the next call, they explained that during a calm ice cream social, Mom got up from her chair, crossed the room and pinched Harry. The nurse on duty called me to say that they had permission from the Director to "send her away." That was a bit frightening. What do they mean—"send her away?" Kicking and screaming, they took her to the Emergency Room.

My thoughts were that Harry might have reminded Mom of my Dad, whom she did grow to hate late in their marriage. Another hypothesis was that she was feeling that Greg was being taken away again and again. The disease is so confusing and explaining any of her behaviors was getting tiresome. I recalled, that when I was growing up, Mom had to feel in control of situations and when things were out of control everyone around her was miserable.

By now Jack and I were living in the hangar while we built out house. The phone rang at 2 am. The clinician on duty in the ER was trying to figure out why she was there. He said she seemed fine to him. Laughing, I said, "but of course- because she is sleeping!" I went on to convey the incidents that had occurred with Greg's death, her disease, and her obsession with Harry. By 6 am, he called back and said they would be taking her by police car to Lewis Gale Allegheny hospital to get her medications stabilized so she would not be so agitated and aggressive. I agreed that this would be best and would come to visit as soon as I could get there.

We had subcontractors coming and going on our construction site and my work with Virginia Tech, I had to determine the best time to leave to go see her. I also needed to go by Wheatland to get her some clothes and underwear before going to visit. While packing at Wheatland, I found an unopened gift that Sherry had mailed her for Mother's Day as well as some other unopened cards. I opened the package to find a really nice spring outfit from Sherry. I took the outfit and the card to Mom. Again, Sherry was desperately was trying from a distance to connect. In her room I found somebody else's shoes, a video that was not ours, someone's Virginia Tech hat in her drawer, and her remote buried in a cabinet. Recalling that residents go "shopping" in each other's rooms, I just donated those items to the lost and found.

After Mom had been in Allegheny for 3 days, I drove to visit. It was about 2 hours away. This is my email update to Mike and Sherry:

~~~~~~~~~~

August 24, 2012
From Karen to Mike & Sherry

I drove to the Lewis Gale Allegheny hospital to see Mom. She had on clean clothes and was glad to see me. We loved on each other while I waited to talk with Dr. K. I turned on Sesame Street on TV and she liked the puppets. She DID not want to go into her assigned room.

When Dr. K came, we tried to talk there but Mom was distracted so we walked to Mom's room. In the doorway, she stopped at the door and didn't want to go in. I don't know why. It was bright and clean but maybe that is where they struggled with her bath.

Dr. K was nice. He said that the CBT (Cognitive Behavioral Program) that Wheatland was recommending would not be a good alternative with someone with such dementia as she has. He was changing her meds to Depakot to give her a higher dosage at bedtime and less in the mornings. He recommended weaning her off Seroquil and asked about changing from her Exelon patch (for memory) to Namenda. She had been on Namenda before and I asked him to call the neurologist to discuss that with him.

One thing that concerned me was sending her

back to Wheatland Hills in the same situation where she had not been successful. I asked Dr. K about alternatives. A program that the doc told me about in Roanoke, Virginia was called **Emeritus.** I made a mental note to look into this alternative should she still not be happy at Wheatland.

I went back in to spend some time with Mom and removed her old nail polish but they would not allow me to paint any new polish on since the polish was in a glass bottle. Geez.

On the way home, I called one of Greg's caregivers from the condo. She said she would be willing to go to see Mom two times a week to do her hair, teeth and baths. I agreed to pay Irma for that.

Wheatland Hills says they were planning to go re-evaluate Mom on Monday but that if she were allowed back, we would have to transport her.

There was a great deal of financial business to take care of. On my way home from my visit with Mom, I talked with her long-term care insurance representative (Allianz) to clear up an issue with a disbursement. The check for Mom's reimbursement this month was about $1500-$2000 less than usual. After talking with Wheatland, they discovered that for the month of June, they had mixed up Margaret Gregory with another Margaret. So indeed, they owe us the balance. This afternoon, Debra the Director called back indicating that they had reviewed Mom's financial billing and that they had mixed up these two women since November and that we owe Wheatland over $7000 for their mistake. I told her to send me a record of what they submitted and what it should have been. I had to compare this report to the check stubs I had filed. Oh my goodness! In addition, I have been on the phone and mailing POAs to the State of Virginia, BCBS, and Medco Prescription Plan, and Medicare. Minding Mom's finances is a fulltime business!

~~~~~~~~~~

Mom spent two weeks in Allegheny. Wheatland evaluated her once and was not yet willing to take her back. That's when I began thinking about not sending her back to Wheatland. I recalled that the doctor at Allegheny had mentioned a memory care hospital called Emeritus in Roanoke. Roanoke would be closer for me but slightly further for Mike and Lisa.

I figured that I needed a back-up plan. On Wednesday, August 29, I called Emeritus to see if I might come visit and look at the facility. I met the Community Relations Director, Susan. She was a (Virginia Tech) Hokie, which was good news from the beginning. But better than that, the program, called "Join Their Journey" really resonated with me. Rather than one long hallway and a dining room as in Wheatland, there were four pods, a large secured courtyard, and interesting activities spread throughout the facility. There were four levels of care depending on the resident's assessed level of dementia and an occupational therapy unit right in the facility. Susan told me that they had one opening. What a Godsend!

I outlined Mom's history and current medical situation noting that she was in Allegheny. Once I toured the facility I had the feeling that this was the place that Mom needed to be. Susan said that they were headed to Allegheny that afternoon to assess another potential resident and could drop by to see Mom. Oh my, I sure had a feeling that God was in charge of this move! Susan called later that afternoon. They had assessed Mom at a level 2 and that they could admit her if I wanted. Indeed I did, and set the plan into action to move Mom. First I notified the director of Wheatland that Mom would not be returning and I would pick up her things the next day. I wish I could say they sounded sad, but I really feel they were relieved!

Mike and I met at Wheatland the very next day to pick up what she would need at Emeritus. Marge even came to help and took several things to the thrift shop. She also took Greg's casket flag and planned to give it back to Greg's sons. The "Ham, hm" lady was wandering in and out of Mom's room and Jack gave her a pack of Ritz crackers and just kept telling her to "Go away" which didn't faze her.

We scaled back what she would need since her space would be smaller. We loaded up two pick-up trucks with Mom's remaining belongings. It was somewhat sad to see that her worldly belongings fit into the back of two trucks.

Chapter 8
A New Start in a New Memory Care Location

After leaving Christiansburg, Jack and I went to
Emeritus to set up her room so it would be familiar
the next day when I would pick her up at Alleghany.
We set up her television, put her bedspread on the
bed, and her clothes in the closet. I placed family
photos and her stuffed animals in the room so it
would look like home.

Friday, I traveled to Allegheny to pick up Mom. With
a construction continuing on our house, Jack stayed
on our property to supervise. Mike and Lisa were to
meet me at Emeritus. When I arrived to get her,
Mom was ready and willing to go with me. She was
clean and bathed and got right into the car. On the
2-hour trip, we sang, laughed, and generally had a
good time. She kept holding my hand and telling me
how much she loved me and loved spending time
with me. It was a joyful trip!

Mike met Mom with open arms and we led her to
her new home. She said it was nice and we walked
all around the grounds, spending about 3 hours with
her. We got to know some of the interesting
characters who she would share space with. First of
all the woman who had been moved from of the
room in Level 2 care that Mom was to occupy to
level 3 care wandered in and out of Mom's room
wondering where her new room was. Then there
was the Level 4 woman, Sue, who walked the
grounds all day. She was tall, thin and with only non-
skid socks on. She held her hands out in front of her

body with fists up as she walked as if she was sleep walking but awake.

One woman who looked younger than mom and who looked really physically fit never sat down. She walked in and out and around the halls the whole time we were there. She would walk past saying "Nothing New" and keep walking. That was interspersed with "Let's get outa here." Occasionally she parroted "Nationwide is on your side" or "I need a weight watcher bar." The nurse said that she repeats anything you say.

There was not room for everything we had brought for Mom in her new room. While Mike went to transfer some more of Mom's belongings to my car, Mom and I wandered outside and sat in the gazebo. There was a little man hiding behind a tree. We could see him but he didn't move. I said, "We can see you!" He moved to another tree and we just laughed and laughed. Then here came the parrot, "Nothing new, let's get outa here!" I said, " I like your shirt." She repeated "like your shirt." I said, " Have a seat." She said, "Have a seat." Mom said to tell her to "go to hell." That's where I drew the line. She wandered on and next came another wanderer carrying a man's shirt. This hunched over woman was sweaty from hours of walking and said she needed to walk home and wondered which way to go. I turned her around and headed her back inside. I noticed the nurses later trying to bring her inside to hydrate her.

So all was going according to plan when Mike and Lisa came back and said we needed an exit strategy.

They would leave first. That made Mom none too happy. She started explaining something that was hard to follow. Knowing her voice inflections and what I thought she meant, I interpreted that to mean she just wanted us all to stay together. I told her I had to get home to Jack and Kramer and building our house. She said that I needed to stay there with her. She said, "I don't know these people or what to do." I told her the twin bed wasn't large enough for us both and she said, "It's just you and me." I hated to burst her bubble from the wonderful morning we had experienced together. I engaged a few staff members including Susan, the Community Director, who had come back to check on Mom. She sat with Mom while I left. By this time, Mom was giving me the cold shoulder and not wanting any hugs or kisses. I just left. Every time I had to leave, I was sad as I watched Mom slipping away.

After a few weeks at Emeritus, I noticed that Mom was having a hard time sitting down on the toilet seat. It was as if it was too low and she was afraid to sit all the way down for fear of falling. It took about 10 minutes and 45 tries before she finally did it. She opened the bathroom cabinet door on one try to hold on to it. That's when I found the card Sherry had mailed her. It was under the bathroom sink. She loved the little guardian angel pin Sherry sent but wanted to keep it in the box and not wear it. I asked the staff to get a raised seat for her toilet. (9-6-2012).

On one visit, I noticed Mom had 2 peanut butter crackers in her hand. As we were talking, she laid them on the table. The woman who keept saying, "nothing new" came up and just took mom's cracker right off the table and ate it. Mom didn't seem to care. We stayed a little over an hour mostly reviewing her photo album. She seemed to recall much of it...amazing! It made me cry for her memory loss. And each time she saw Dad she stroked his picture lovingly. When I cried, she started to cry, so I straightened right up for fear she would lose her calm.

By the end of September (2012), Sherry came to Virginia to check on her house construction. Together, we went to visit mom. Sherry had brought her a nice coral colored sweater and I had planned to do her nails and clean her glasses for her. When we walked in (about 11 am), she was in a foul mood. She recognized us but was

angry. The staff said they had just bathed her. This must be an ordeal. They also said she had had a "tough night." Apparently she is not wiping well after bowel movements and they had to clean her up. She has a little rash as well. When I saw that she was agitated, I went to get her some chocolate and the photo album with black and whites of days past. She ate the chocolate and I offered one to a woman named Alma. It was then that I noticed Alma was wearing Mom's purple velour jogging suit that I got her last Christmas. Residents shopping in each other's rooms again! Offering the chocolate and talking slowly through the photos worked to calm her down. She said she was cold so I offered her the jacket Sherry had brought. She said she didn't need that. I put the jacket on myself. In about 5 minutes, again, she said that she was cold so I took off the new jacket and placed it on her. She liked it then.

We stayed for about an hour while Sherry practiced getting along with the *different* Mom. Sherry is one to continue a conversation by using rapid-fire questions. Mom could no longer keep up with that pace. I painted her nails and trimmed a few (since staff said that during baths she has scratched them). I couldn't clean her glasses because she didn't have them on. I looked (and the staff looked) everywhere for them. I found her prescription sunglasses and brought them to her. She was happy with that. I know that optometrists can measure the glasses prescription and I could get more glasses using those glasses if I needed to. I mentioned the missing glasses to Kim, the nurse. When I called the next day, they had been located.

It is always better to give her something to do when we leave, so leaving her at the table at lunch seemed like a good exit strategy which is what we did that day. But not before Sherry shed tears, tears that I have already shed many a time, over the loss of our "mama."

In December, Lisa, Sherry, and I decided it was time for a field trip. We took mom to Sweet Frogs for frozen yogurt. She loved it and consumed two bowls. She still said, "I love you," but she didn't know our names.

That Christmas, I couldn't speak to Mom on the phone or in person. We were visiting Jack's mom in  Tennessee. There were other parts of the family that needed attention as well!

When I returned to visit in January, Mom was asleep. I had noticed that she was sleeping more. I had asked the staff to reduce the anti-psychotic drugs so she wouldn't sleep so much and would be more stable on her feet. We purchased some different, more therapeutic shoes and she liked them. But, her new clothes were gone and her pretty bedspread was gone. She had unrecognizable bedding on her bed.

We continued to work on building our house as did Sherry and Mike. We all wanted to live close to each other and share in Mom's care. We continued to share what we were learning and stroke each other in the process, like this message from Mike:
~~~~~~~~~~

May 2013

Karen that last email was so well stated. I can feel your heartbreak through your words. She remains a wonderful Mom who taught us the importance of real love. Thanks for your continued care of Mom and her assets; you truly carry the larger burden of Mom's care. Most of all we do have a wonderful family, I am so proud of all of our kids that have fought their way into legitimate adult hood. Love to all.

From: Karen
Sent: Fri, May 10, 2013 1:53 pm
Subject: Letter to Mom
****

Dear Family-
On Facebook, I see everyone posting Happy Mother's Day to their Mom's and others for the weekend. So I am wishing each of you, who are mothers, Happy Mother's Day as well. Do you know what a great family we have? And what great kids the next generation of you are becoming? This week, Tony asked me for the address where Mom lives to send her something for Mother's Day. Destiny called me too and ended up writing a heartfelt message that

Whitney packed up to send to Mom. It breaks my heart to tell you that she won't be able to connect the dots to know it is from you, but she will feel the love and of that I am certain.

I visited Mom on Wednesday this week. It was a good visit but the staff says she will be moved up a level of care (meaning she is declining). Staff was busy, so I didn't get the specifics. She is in level 2 now and there are 4 levels of care as her condition degrades. I helped her toilet and change her pants. She has put on weight because eating seems to be the most important part of her life. I took her some candy and she loved it. Even though it's not the best for her with weight gain and nutrition, I love the look on her face when she tastes it. She has always loved chocolate!

Today, I had to stop and gather my thoughts about mom and wrote down just because that helps me with clarity. I wanted to share some thoughts and my perspectives with you. I welcome your stories this Mother's Day weekend as well.

~~~~~~

Mom-Mother's Day 2013
Even though she doesn't know my name
I can see it in her eyes that she loves me.
For many years, I had to think up special gifts to
show my love. But
now gifts mean little.
She even has difficulty figuring out how to open
a package.

She is still alive and for that I am thankful. She
doesn't know it's
Mothers Day. She doesn't know that March 22
was her 83rd birthday or
that March 7th was my birthday. She doesn't
know that she has grand
children and great grand children who are
making an effort to reach
out to her this Mother's Day.

She can't tell you who the President of the
United States is or the
name of her daddy. But she still can show
emotions; she has a twinkle
in her eye and a dance in her step. She calls me
(and about anyone
else) "baby."

She taught me to be proactive and organized.
She taught me to complete
tasks and be honest. Not all aspects about her
were positive. She held grudges, she angered
easily, and she had some biases. But it is even
through those examples that I learned how to
form my own values.

One thing I do know is she would fight tooth and
nail for the rights

of her children and work really hard to sustain important relationships. I miss my mom and who she was. I honor her for facing Alzheimer's with honor and dignity and only hope that someday I can look in the face of Cancer like my Dad did... with strength; or look into the face of Alzheimer's with the ability to continue to step one foot in front of the other and still smile and call strangers "baby."
Love ya, Mom. Your Karen
~~~~~~~

Chapter 9
Life in Assisted Living - Level 3 and 4

In June, I met with the assisted living staff to discuss mom's care. They announced that she has gained 17 lbs. she now weighs 158. I knew I had to purchase larger clothes! They said that now they use more gestures to get her to do things (like eat, put on sock) since she can't understand the meaning of many words and that is frustrating for her. The staff now spends more time with her on daily tasks such as toileting, especially to reduce incidence of UTIs, which are prevalent among those who sit a lot and who can't properly wipe. They take more time to get her ready each day. Her ability to ambulate has not changed. She is level 3 out of 4 now but this is where they plan to keep her for now. I took Pull-ups and Sherry brought her new pants when we visited.

We are full into house construction. That sure keeps us busy on the home front!

In August, 2013, I sent an email to the family with the subject line, *"Grandmommy's Foot."* Sounding like it could be the title of a children's book, I explained that it was just our maternal flesh and blood screaming bloody murder! About 3 weeks ago when Sherry was visiting, we went to see Mom. Lisa and Mike joined us. The PT staff had called asking if we could bring her some tennis shoes instead of the slip-on she was wearing. She wanted nothing to do with the shoes when I showed them to her 3 different times over the course of 10 minutes. We went to get the Physical Therapy gal that she seemed like. She got the shoes on but not without the shrillest shriek you ever heard. All the other residents started getting agitated and asking what was wrong and "to get her outa here." Once the shoe was on, she was ok. It was like night and day behavior. The PT said the toe was BLACK! That had shocked Mike who was thinking amputation. But we soon realized it was the toenail not the toe!

We scheduled an appointment with the podiatrist. I decided to take her but enlisted Mike and Lisa's help. Getting her in the car was a bit of an (slow) ordeal and her perception must have been off since she was afraid when cars pass and when they slide over in the lane ahead of us. We got to the Doc's office 10 minutes early and it was still closed for lunch at 12:50. I had brought a photo album so we sat in the car and looked at pictures. At 1:00, Lisa forged the way, while Mike and I maneuvered her out of the car. I had called ahead so they were prepared for her "condition" and potential screaming.

She went to the exam room and refused to recline in the podiatrist chair. She sat on the edge. Lisa stayed in the waiting room. Mike and I situated ourselves in chairs nearby. Since she would not lean back in the chair, the doctor sat on the floor to work on her toe. With a snip, snip the toenail was off. But not without some blood curdling screams. I held her hands from scratching the doctor and Mike anchored her left leg from kicking. Lisa explained to the people in the waiting room what was going on, and then Mom appears afterwards all smiles as if nothing had happened.

It went far better than we expected. Once back at Emeritus, we gave her a cookie and a piece of chocolate, settled her in her reclining chair for a nap, and departed. Phew!

September-December, 2014

In September, we started giving a hard push towards being finished with our house that would also become Bedford Landings Bed & Breakfast. We wanted to be open for business by December in hopes we would get a tax break. During this time, I was still working at Virginia Tech but we were also wiring, plumbing, undergoing inspections and literally working 12-hour days. One Sunday, I did a stupid thing. I was on the newly constructed deck and slipped and fell through the front porch joists where the boards were not screwed down yet. I had to call for help to get up but thought I was ok. I kept pushing ahead and working but after 4 weeks, Jack insisted that I see a doctor since I was limping and swinging my leg out to walk. They X-rayed and said it was muscular, prescribing me a powerful steroid. After ten days, I returned to the doctor to see what other suggestions they had since that had not made anything change. They sent me for an MRI. The results came back before I had driven home from Lynchburg (45 minutes away) and the diagnosis was a broken hip. There were two cracks in the femur. The doc wanted me to get 2 screws surgically inserted. But when would I do that? I was working at Tech, building a house, traveling when I could to see Mom and trying to juggle many things.

The Orthopedist's convincing argument was that I could step off of a ladder and the femur could break all of the way through and break entirely. Then I would be looking at an artificial hip, not just two screws! On Halloween, Jack and I went to Lynchburg and I had the surgery. I guess I was on crutches for about a week, in bed for about 2 days then back to work! I was staining all of the woodwork supported

on sawhorses. Jack was wiring the entire house, and our friends and family were all rallying helping us!

We moved into the new house on December 10th and opened for business December 17th. Phew! I had decided against physical therapy thinking that moving and settling was enough exercise. But it wasn't. I needed intentional movements to re-learn to walk straight. So from January to March, I went about 3 times a week to work the limp out of my walking.

Mom continued to gain weight, dance, and sing when we would sing with her. She watched our lips and mimicked the words as they *sort* of came back to her. She was moody, but less so. Generally, when I would enter the room to visit, she was napping in her chair. She could not seem to do anything else. The staff kept the TV on but the staff was no longer attempting other activities. I guess the mental connections aren't there anymore to understand WHY to make something, stir something, sort, draw or hardly even converse. She enjoyed music and Jack and I took her to a concert in the community room where they were singing "In Her Easter Bonnet." She laughed and hummed along! When I left that day, I did one of my spontaneous interpretive dances out the door. All the residents looked at me as if I was loony, but Mom just smiled broadly and waved!

Mom doesn't seem to remember what to do with food. The staff recommended cutting her food into bite-sized pieces (finger food) to help her eat. Several times the staff had found it necessary to "clear her mouth" as she packed food in her jaws like a squirrel, not knowing how to swallow. Not a good sign.

By March (2014), the staff reported that they were mashing Mom's food. She was still ambulatory and up everyday and dressed. I tried to make the trip to see her about every other week; sometimes every week. Each time that I went to campus at Virginia Tech, I stopped in to see Mom. In my area working with Cooperative Extension, Human Development, I had responsibility for developing teaching materials and holding in-service education sessions for all Extension Agents in the state regarding any aspect of the age spectrum for human development. I was involved in an intergenerational grant, working with projects across the state, conducting training, and also was asked to be interim Associate Director of Family and Consumer Sciences for the state. I worked mostly from home at all hours and I traveled to Blacksburg only when necessary.

In April (2014), Mom was moved to Level 4 in Emeritus. The residents were all rather quiet and just slept in their chairs or beds. It smelled of feces but I think they were keeping it as clean as possible. Mom was wearing an adult diaper and still knew where her room was but they staff were saying she was weaker and they needed to escort her (one on each side) to her room each time she wanted to lay down. There were few to no activities for residents.

By May, the Emeritus staff recommended that we consider Hospice. I always thought Hospice was for bedridden patients who were dying. They must have known something about this process that I didn't know. Medicare covers Hospice. Hospice will give her meds if she is in pain but she didn't seem to be in pain. I made an appointment to discuss this with them.

I did some research to find out how exactly one dies of Alzheimer's. What I learned was basically they forget how to do everything that sustains them; eating, toileting, digesting, and eventually breathing. As I drove to visit Mom one day, I sadly, was at a loss for what to offer her. I stopped at a gas station store and picked up some prepared smoothie drinks. The staff (nurse assistants) said she was not eating so I was thinking about what she liked. She has always liked smoothies and milk shakes. Once I was there, I found her in her chair in her room. I offered her a sip and she took a few sips through a straw. She seems so tired. I asked her if she wanted to lie down. She did. Then I crawled in bed next to her. I whispered and talked in her ear and we lay there like two schoolgirls having a sleep over.

I told her stories about her life and each person in our family and what they were doing. I told her about how the family would soon come together for one of her grand daughter's wedding. I told her that our house was now completed and that we have started running the Bed & Breakfast business.

We sang and cuddled. She cried and I stroked her and caressed her. It was a special time for us. A few days later when Jack and I visited, she said, "Kids come see me." I thought, "What?" She hadn't made much verbal sense in some time and she was asking about the grand children. So I said, "Let me see what I can do about that!" Mom had five grand children. The "kids" ranged in age from 24-40. The oldest, Tony lived in Colorado. The other four, Katie, Garrett, Whitney and Shawn lived in Raleigh, NC. We indeed let the kids come to see her. From Colorado to North Carolina, we used Skype, FaceTime, Google Hangout, and the cell phone so each grandchild and great grandchild could tell Mom how much they loved her. Reflecting on it later, this was important to her letting go. It gave her permission and reassured her that we were all ok and she knew it was time to leave us.

On May 22, Whitney decided that she wanted to come see Mom in person. I thought I would lose it when I saw what she had brought. She pulled out her "white blanket" which was Whitney's childhood comfort item. She laid it on Mom's shoulder. We tried to give her what the nurses called "red thick liquid," which is some sort of nutrition concoction. It just rolled out of her mouth and some of it got on the white blanket. We stayed about 2 hours. Whitney later posted this on Facebook:
~~~~~~~~~

"Today was a first for me, I encountered the most difficult thing I've ever done...to turn around & walk out of my grandmother's room being completely aware of the fact that it would be the last time I see her alive. But I thank the Lord for letting me have that chance & for blessing her with the chance to hear all of her grandchildren's voices & sweet wishes over the phone. Despite being an emotional wreck, I did intensely pay attention to her very slight reactions to the things we said to her. Tony Hume, she may have not said a word back but I could see a look in her eyes & I know her heart was smiling. Shawn Patrick, I showed her a video of Jamison & with lots of effort, she moved her hand as if she wanted to touch the screen & say one of her cute comments. Katie & Garrett Brown, I don't know how your conversations went with her the other day but we talked about you guys today & even though she wasn't able to verbally acknowledge anything, I know it put her mind more at ease to finally hear everyone's voice.

Ted DeBord, we talked about you as well...she has been having little tremors in her mouth & hands and when we mentioned you, the tremors stopped for a few seconds as if she was acknowledging us. I am so, so grateful to have had my momma, Karen DeBord by my side throughout today. No words in the world can even begin to explain how much you mean to me. And with the little reach for your hand that Grandmom did before we left today, made me think that maybe she was trying to thank you & let you know that everything is going to be ok. Life isn't meant to be easy, It's meant to be lived, to the fullest. And that is for sure what Margaret Brown accomplished. We love her so very, very much & will forever remember how wonderfully loving & amazing she was to all of us."

~~~~~~~~

Before Whitney and I left that day, I held mom's hand, caressed her, hugged her and I felt her tighten the grip on my hand. I told her that she had now seen all of the children and she could let go. I said, "You have been a wonderful Mom and friend but now you need to go be with Jesus and sit with him. We will miss you terribly!"

The next morning, as I was driving to get an oil change in the car, I got the call that she would probably die that morning. By this time, I was carrying my folder with her will and funeral plans in my car. I did a U-turn and went straight to Emeritus. I called Mike and Sherry along the way. Mike started preparing to meet me there and apparently fell in the shower, as he was getting ready. Poor guy! She was dead and laying in the bed when we got there. I called McCoy Funeral Home to come to pick up her body. The Hospice representative offered to put clean underwear and pants on her. After she was cleaned up by Hospice, we touched her and talked to her, standing by her bed in disbelief. When the funeral director picked her up, her body was already stiff as a board and he seemed to lift her effortlessly to put her on the gurney to wheel her away.

Mom's Efficiency Realized Ever After her Death
Mom had made many decisions, which I so appreciated that day. She had selected her casket, paid for the funeral and the grave plot. She had listed pallbearers and friends to notify. Most of these arrangements, she made BEFORE she had Alzheimer's. How did she know? I have no clue, but it's a lesson I heeded. Later that month, I purchased Long Term Care insurance, as did my sister and brother. I paid for my funeral and purchased my graveyard plot at Bethlehem United Methodist Church in Moneta, VA. Even in her death, she was organized and her papers, her will, her small

investments and her funeral had already been considered.

Moms had many special friends and most who were in town were able to come to serve as pall bearers (women and men). One person who Mom had requested in her planning papers was Coach Beamer. He had a complex recruiting trip to California planned and could not cancel it. He kindly checked in with me about 3 times to apologize, sent flowers, and made a donation to the Alzheimer's Foundation. Cheryl, his sweet wife, who mom also loved, attended as did the Gabbards (Mom and Greg's wedding witnesses), Marge, Courtney and so many others who said many nice things and told stories about her!

Mike, Sherry and I spoke at her funeral. Here is what I said:
~~~~~~~~~~
Today, I say goodbye to the efficient, organized, loving Mom who raised me several years ago. As many of you know, she spent the last few years in Assisted Living, a victim of Alzheimer's disease.

At first it was funny; a forgotten word or a funny pairing of terms. But in the end, it was just sad that she could not express what she would have wanted to say; and many of you know she was never short of words!

Today, I choose to remember my Mom who went outside with me after dinner to play ball, who taught me to read a recipe and to sew. I remember *that* Mom who tried to teach me to play bridge and taught me to make snow cream and play Tripoly. She blessed me with a sister and brother. But then as we wrestled with each other growing up, she also drummed into our heads: *"Sweetness begets sweetness"* and *"If you can't say anything nice, don't say anything at all!"*

I loved sharing a glass (or 2) of wine sitting on the carport swing at 1418 Locust or with her or later with Mom and Greg on the deck at Chateau Court.

While I was also working at Virginia Tech in the 90's, I would drive to work and already see her car parked near the Coliseum by 7:30 each morning. Mom was a true Hokie. And she had the wardrobe, jewelry, hats and pins to prove it.

She was proud to support the Football coaches and many others in the Athletic department; and we love that you too, looked after her!

Ten days ago, I crawled up beside her in her bed at Emeritus and told her stories about her life and each person in our family. She cried and I stroked her and caressed her. It was a special time for us. A few days later, she said, "Kids come see me." And indeed each grandchild told Mom how much he or she loved her. This was important to her letting go. It gave her permission and reassured her that we were all ok and she knew it was time to leave us.

Thank-you each, for being her friend. Thanks ever-steady friends Marge and Travis, thanks, David for singing one of Mom's favorite hymns. Entitled, *Fill my Cup Lord,* it was written by my grand parent's pastor years ago. And thanks to those she asked to be her pallbearers because she loved you. Thanks for loving her back!

Mom's earthly conversation with GOD now becomes a heavenly and glorious eternity. We rejoice that she is can now gain clarity on many of the questions of life.

We may have enjoyed a glass of wine with her here on earth but who do you think is "filling her cup" now?" Hallelujah!

Family Time After the Funeral

Mom is buried in Roselawn Cemetery between Blacksburg and Christiansburg, VA next to her parents Laura Sue Clamon Grindstaff and Charles Coleman Grindstaff. At the graveside, Jack played bagpipes while the funeral attendants laid Mom to rest.

Following the funeral, we had about 15 family members checking into a hotel. We had already made reservations but the front desk clerk said the rooms were not ready yet. Mom would have been proud of us exercising our consumer rights as we went ahead and took over the lobby and made ourselves at home, passing around food and corking wine. The manager kindly moved us to a large ballroom, which was perfect. We sent out for food, did chair races, challenged each other to relays, played football indoors and generally worked off several days worth of emotional energy. Again, Mom would have been proud as our family did what it does best to deal with stress...sit around and cry? No, hold up a glass, make a toast, and then move on.

The Clamon genes bring with them a fiery energy that seems to drive us, makes us strong and keeps up moving forward anticipating our next great achievement. Mom was a legacy that will live on in our little ones forever. Each person managed Mom's death with dignity. We are so fortunate that she passed that on to us...and for that we thank her!

Epilogue

When your parent dies, you are no longer the child. You become the new generation parent! We cared for Mom over a seven-year period, from her initial diagnosis until her death. I remain proud and overwhelmed by the organized grace with which she lived and died.

As Mom would have wanted, Sherry, Karen and Mike continue to work to fulfill the generational role of patriarch or matriarch. Five years after Mom died, we continue to get together for special family time! Thanksgiving is generally our special holiday since there are so many demands on families during Christmas. Every family member is unique and working hard to be self-sufficient and independent. There have been marriages and divorces, births, and job changes. This family photo was taken in 2018 of our mix and match family.

And yes, Sweetness does beget sweetness!

Photo Index

Page 6 Mom as a little girl, she looks to be about 6 years old.

Page 7 Mom and Betty Jo Kress , looks to be about 11 years old

Page 8 Mom's high school graduation photo (age 18)

Page 9 Mom with the backdrop of East Tennessee State University, in college

Page 10 Mom and Dad's wedding day

Page 11 Family Photo in Emory, circa 1963. Mom would have been 33 years old

Page 12 Mom and Dad in front of the Emory house, circa 1964

Page 14 Grandmother, Bookey and Mom, probably in the 70's

Page 19 Mom and Coach Frank Beamer, probably around 1989

Page 22 Mom and high school sweetheart Bud Bullis, circa 2000. Take on the carport at the Locust Avenue house in Blacksburg

Page 24 Mom and Greg's wedding photo about 2004.

Page 27- Mom in her red hat. This is the photo that we displayed at the funeral.

Page 27 Mike, Sherry, John, Jack (l to R standing), Lisa and Karen (seated), 2006 preparing for Mom's surprise birthday scavenger hunt

Page 29 – Mom matching socks, 2007

Page 35- Mom dressed up and Mom on the deck of the Vistas condo

Page 36 – Mom and Greg walking in St. Petersburg, FL

Page 63- Mom at Wheatland Hills with some residents, 2012

Page 120 - Mom's gravestone at Roselawn Cemetery in Blacksburg, VA

Page 121- Family Photo taken at Thanksgiving 2018. From the top

John (Sherry's husband), Mike, Quentin (Whitney's husband), Shawn with baby Zahra, Tianna (Zahra's mom), Jack, Lisa, Garrett, Whitney, Megan (Tony's wife), Tony

Ashley, Kendall (Garrett's daughter), Katie with baby Emma Grace (Garrett's child), Sherry

Lyla & Jaylyn (Garret's daughters), Karen, Destiny

Credits: Many thanks to Kathy Grost Sargent for assisting with final editing.

Made in the USA
Columbia, SC
11 March 2019